ACSL Contests 2019-2020

The comprehensive and authoritative collection of the 2019-2020 competitions organized by the American Computer Science League

Carlen Blackstone
Marc Brown
Janice Meegan
Gerald Tebrow

ACSL Contests 2019-2020

The comprehensive and authoritative collection of the 2019-2020 competitions organized by the American Computer Science League

Carlen Blackstone
Marc Brown
Janice Meegan
Gerald Tebrow

Published by the Association of Computer Science Leagues, Inc.

ISBN: 978-1-71662-313-4

CONTENTS

Introduction

This book contains the 2019-2020 contests organized by the American Computer Science League. ACSL is divided into 5 divisions: Senior, Intermediate, Junior, Elementary, and Classroom. The competitions in the Senior, Intermediate, and Junior divisions consist of two parts: *short problems* that cover fundamental concepts in computer science and a *programming problem* that students solve by writing a computer program in a language of their choice. The Elementary and Classroom divisions consist of short problems only.

The topics covered in the short problems are as follows:

Assembly Language Programming
Bit-String Flicking
Boolean Algebra
Computer Number Systems
Data Structures
Digital Electronics
FSAs and Regular Expressions
Graph Theory
LISP
Prefix/Infix/Postfix Notation
Recursive Functions
What Does This Program Do?

The topics are described in **categories.acsl.org,** along with example problems and lots of teaching and learning resources.

ACSL organizes four regular-season contests, held at each participating school. At the end of the season, in pre-pandemic times, the top-scoring schools would be invited to participate in an All-Star Contest held at one of the participating schools. In 2019-2020, the season culminated with top-scoring students invited to participate in an online Finals competition. The results of the regular season and of the Finals are available at **leaderboard.acsl.org/2020**.

ACSL was established in 1978 to provide high school computer science education through computer science competitions. It has been organizing monthly contests and an end-of-year invitational competition continuously since then. ACSL welcomes participation from pre-college schools and organizations from around the world. Please visit our website for more information, **www.acsl.org**.

This book is organized contest by contest. In each contest, the problems and solutions are organized by division. Sample solutions to the programming problems are not printed here; the online leaderboard has links to student-written solutions in various computer languages (typically, Python, Java, and C/C++). Please report any errors to **www.acsl.org/book-bugs** so they can be corrected in future printings of this book.

We hope you enjoy solving these problems as much as we enjoyed creating them.

ACSL 2020 Executive Team

Carlen Blackstone
Marc Brown
Janice Meegan
Gerald Tebrow

Contest #1

American Computer Science League

2019-2020 — **Contest #1**

SENIOR DIVISION

1. Computer Number Systems Evaluate and express the answer in hex: $(42_8) * (42_8)$	**1.**
2. Computer Number Systems Tickets to a play were numbered sequentially starting at 100_{10}. A ticket that contains the sequence "1010" when the number is converted to binary is free. If 100 tickets were sold at $5.00 each, what was the income from the tickets?	**2.**
3. Recursive Functions Find f(31) given: ([x] = greatest integer <= x) $f(x) = \begin{cases} f([x/2]-5)+4 & \text{if } x >= 8 \\ f(x+2) - 2^\wedge x & \text{if } x <= 4 \\ x - 4 & \text{otherwise} \end{cases}$	**3.**

American Computer Science League

2019-2020 — **Contest #1**

SENIOR DIVISION

4. Recursive Functions Find f(2, 16, 8) if given: $$f(x, y, z) = \begin{cases} f(x + 1, y - 4, z) + x * z & \text{if } y >= 7 \\ f(x - 2, y + 1, z - 2) - x * y & \text{if } 4 <= y < 7 \\ x + y + z & \text{if } y < 4 \end{cases}$$	**4.**
Question #5 is on the next page.	

American Computer Science League

2019-2020 Contest #1

SENIOR DIVISION

5.

5. What Does This Program Do?

What is outputted when this program is executed?

```
a = 20: b = 4
c = a / b
if a / b < a / c then
   d = b + c
end if
d = c - b
if b ^ d > c ^ d then
    e = b + d
else
    e = c + d
end if
f = a - b * c + d ^ e
if (c * e - a < 0) || (d - f < 0) then
    d = 2 * d
else
    f = 3 * f
end if
if (a / e > f) && (a / f < c) then
    b = e - c
end if
a = e * f - b
if (a - b < 2 * c) || ((b = c - d) && (e > f)) then
    f = b + d - c
end if
g = (a + b) / e + c
h = a / (d + e) * b * g / b ^ 2 - c ^ f + 4 * ((c + d) / (e - b)) ^ (g / b)
print h
end
```

American Computer Science League

2019-2020 — **Contest #1**

SENIOR DIVISION SOLUTIONS

1. Computer Number Systems $42_8 = 34_{10}$ $34 * 34 = 1156 = 484_{16}$	**1.** 484_{16} or 484
2. Computer Number Systems 100 tickets @$5.00 = $500.00 $100_{10} = 1100100_2$ and $199_{10} = 11000111_2$ Tickets numbered 104, 105, 106, 107, 116, 117, 122, 138, 148, 149, 154, 160 - 175 (16 #'s), 180, 181, and 186 contain the sequence "1010". Income = $500 - 30 * $5 = $500 - $150 = $350.	**2.** $ 350 or 350
3. Recursive Functions f(31) = f([31/2] - 5) + 4 = f(15-5) + 4 = f(10) + 4 = -15 + 4 = -11 f(10) = f([10/2] - 5) + 4 = f(5 - 5) + 4 = f(0) + 4 = -19 + 4 = -15 f(0) = f(0 + 2) - 2^0 = f(2) + 1 = -18 - 1 = -19 f(2) = f(2 + 2) - 2^2 = f(4) + 4 = -14 - 4 = -18 f(4) = f(4 + 2) - 2^4 = f(6) - 16 = 2 - 16 = -14 f(6) = 6 - 4 = 2	**3.** -11
4. Recursive Functions f(2, 16, 8) = f(2 + 1, 16 - 4, 8) + 2 * 8 = f(3, 12, 8) + 16 = 18 + 16 = 34 f(3, 12, 8) = f(3 + 1, 12 - 4, 8) + 3 * 8 = f(4, 8, 8) + 24 = -6 + 24 = 18 f(4, 8, 8) = f(4 + 1, 8 - 4, 8) + 4 * 8 = f(5, 4, 8) + 32 = -38 + 32 = -6 f(5, 4, 8) = f(5 - 2, 4 + 1, 8 - 2) - 5 * 4 = f(3, 5, 6) - 20 = -18 - 20 = -38 f(3, 5, 6) = f(3 - 2, 5 + 1, 6 - 2) - 3 * 5 = f(1, 6, 4) - 15 = -3 - 15 = -18 f(1, 6, 4) = f(1 - 2, 6 + 1, 4 - 2) - 1 * 6 = f(-1, 7, 2) - 6 = 3 - 6 = -3 f(-1, 7, 2) = f(-1 + 1, 7 - 4, 2) + (-1) * 2 = f(0, 3, 2) - 2 = 5 - 2 = 3 f(0, 3, 2) = 0 + 3 + 2 = 5	**4.** 34

American Computer Science League

2019-2020 Contest #1

SENIOR DIVISION SOLUTIONS

5. What Does This Program Do?

a	b	c	d	e	f	g
20	4	5				
20	4	5	1			
20	4	5	1	6		
20	4	5	1	6	1	
20	4	5	1	6	3	
20	4	5	1	6	3	
14	4	5	1	6	3	
14	4	5	1	6	0	
14	4	5	1	6	0	8

h = a / (d + e) * b * g / b ^ 2 - c ^ f + 4 * ((c + d) / (e - b)) ^ (g / b)
= 14 /(1 + 6)*4*8/4^2 - 5^0 + 4*((5+1)/(6-2))^(8/4)
= 14/7*4*8/16 - 1 + 4*(6/2)^2
= 2*4*8/16 - 1 + 4*3^2
= 8*8/16 - 1 + 36
= 64/16 - 1 +36
= 4 - 1 + 36
= 39

5. 39

AMERICAN COMPUTER SCIENCE LEAGUE

2019-2020 **Contest #1**

Senior Division - Number Transformation

PROBLEM: Given a positive integer (call it N) and a position in that integer (call it P) transform N. To transform N, find the Pth digit of N from the right:

- Replace each of the digits to the left by the sum of that digit and the Pth digit.
- Replace each of the digits to the right by the absolute value of the difference between it and the Pth digit.
- Replace the Pth digit by the number of different prime factors of N. Note that 1 is not a prime number, and it has no prime factors. A prime number has exactly one prime factor (namely, itself).

Example 1: N=102438, P=3. There are 4 different prime factors of N (2, 3, 7, 271). The transformed value N is (1+4)(0+4)(2+4)(4)(|3-4|)(|8-4|) => 5 4 6 4 1 4 => 546414

Example 2: N=4329, P=1. There are 3 different prime factors of N (3, 13, 37). The transformed value of N is (4+9)(3+9)(2+9)(3) => 13 12 11 3 => 1312113

INPUT: There will be 5 sets of data. Each set contains two positive integers: N and P. N will be less than 10^{15} , and P will be valid.

OUTPUT: The transformed value of each input set. The printed number may not have any spaces between the digits.

SAMPLE INPUT: (http://www.datafiles.acsl.org/2020/contest1/sr-sample-input.txt)

```
102438 3
4329   1
6710   2
16807   1
60098065452    7
```

SAMPLE OUTPUT:

1. 546414
2. 1312113
3. 7841
4. 8131571
5. 1488173823436

AMERICAN COMPUTER SCIENCE LEAGUE

2019-2020 **Contest #1**

Senior Division - Number Transformation

TEST DATA

TEST INPUT:

```
43287 3
72431685 1
246897531573 12
96783 5
16058314729 3
```

TEST OUTPUT:

1. 65365
2. 12798611133
3. 424675311351
4. 23216
5. 8137121510811152

American Computer Science League

2019-2020 — **Contest #1**

INTERMEDIATE DIVISION

1. Computer Number Systems Convert 2019_{10} to octal. Write the octal digits in ascending order. Convert this new octal to hex.	**1.**
2. Computer Number Systems Which of the following has the fewest number of 1's in its binary representation? a) 4765_8 b) ABE_{16} c) 8271_{10} d) 1011111011_2	**2.**
3. Recursive Functions Find f(f(f(f(-5)))) given: $f(x)= \begin{cases} f(x + 3) - 2 & \text{if } x < 4 \\ f(2x - 1) + 1 & \text{if } 4 <= x <= 6 \\ x - 4 & \text{if } x > 6 \end{cases}$	**3.**
4. Recursive Functions Given: f(1) = 3 f(2) = 5 f(n) = 3 * f(n - 1) - f(n - 2) Find the smallest value of n such that f(n) > 200.	**4.**

American Computer Science League

2019-2020 — Contest #1

INTERMEDIATE DIVISION

5. What Does This Program Do?

What is outputted when this program is executed?

```
a = 20: b = 4: c = 10: d = 2
if a < b then
    e = b - a
else
    f = a + b
end if
if b + c < a * a then
    b = b + c
else
    d = 2 * c
end if
if c > b && a < d then
    f = b + e
else
    e = f - c
end if
if a + d < b - c || f < d + c then
    a = e
else
    b = f
end if
if a * a < e * e || f > d then
    b = d * d
else
    d = a * a
end if
if b - a  > d - a then
    a = b
else
    b = f
end if
x =  (f / (a + d) - f / (b * d) + (e + d)/(a * b))^((f - e)/d)
print x
end
```

5.

American Computer Science League

2019-2020 — **Contest #1**

INTERMEDIATE DIVISION SOLUTIONS

1. Computer Number Systems

$2019_{10} = 3743_8$

Written in ascending octal digits: 3347_8

$3347_8 = 11\ 011\ 100\ 111_8$

$= 110\ 1110\ 0111_{16}$

$= 6 \quad E \quad 7_{16}$

1. $6E7_{16}$ or 6E7

2. Computer Number Systems

Convert each to binary:

a) $4765_8 = 100111110101_2$ — 8 1's

b) $ABE_{16} = 101010111110_2$ — 8 1's

c) $8271_{10} = 10000001001111_2$ — 6 1's

d) 1011111011_2 — 8 1's

2. 8271_{10} or 8271

3. Recursive Functions

f(-5) = f(-5 + 3) - 2 = f(-2) - 2 = 0 - 2 = -2

f(-2) = f(-2 + 3) - 2 = f(1) - 2 = 2 - 2 = 0

f(1) = f(1 + 3) - 2 = f(4) - 2 = 4 - 2 = 2

f(4) = f(2*4-1) + 1 = f(7) + 1 = 3 + 1 = 4

f(7) = 7 - 4 = 3

f(0) = f(0 + 3) - 2 = f(3) - 2 = 6 - 2 = 4

f(3) = f(3 + 3) - 2 = f(6) - 2 = 8 - 2 = 6

f(6) = f(2*6 - 1) + 1 = f(11) + 1 = 7 + 1 = 8

f(11) = 11 - 4 = 7

So f(f(f(f(-5)))) = f(f(f(-2)))

= f(f(0))

= f(4)

= 4

3. 4

American Computer Science League

2019-2020 Contest #1

INTERMEDIATE DIVISION SOLUTIONS

4. Recursive Functions

f(1) = 3
f(2) = 5
f(3) = 3 * f(2) - f(1) = 3 * 5 - 3 = 12
f(4) = 3 * f(3) - f(2) = 3 * 12 - 5 = 31
f(5) = 3 * f(4) - f(3) = 3 * 31 - 12 = 81
f(6) = 3 * f(5) - f(4) = 3 * 81 - 31 = 212 > 200

4. 6

5. What Does This Program Do?

a	b	c	d	e	f
20	4	10	2		
20	4	10	2		24
20	14	10	2		24
20	14	10	2	14	24
20	24	10	2	14	24
20	4	10	2	14	24
4	4	10	2	14	24

x = (f / (a + d) - f / (b * d) + (e + d)/(a * b))^((f - e)/d)
= (24/(4 + 2) - 24 /(4 * 2) + (14 + 2)/(4 * 4))^((24 - 14)/2)
= (24/6 - 24/8 + 16/16)^(10/2)
= (4 - 3 + 1)^5
= 2^5 = 32

5. 32

AMERICAN COMPUTER SCIENCE LEAGUE

2019-2020 **Contest #1**

Intermediate Division - Number Transformation

PROBLEM: Given a positive integer (call it N) and a position in that integer (call it P) transform N. To transform N, find the Pth digit of N from the right. Replace each of the digits to the left of the Pth digit by the sum of that digit and the Pth digit. If the sum is greater than 9, use just the units digits (see the second example below). Replace each of the digits to the right of the Pth digit by the absolute value of the difference between it and the Pth digit. Do not change the Pth digit.

Example 1: N=102439, P=3. Answer is: (1+4)(0+4)(2+4)4(|3-4|)(|9-4|) => 546415

Example 2: N=4329, P=1. Answer is: (4+9)(3+9)(2+9)9 => (13)(12)(11)9 => 3219

INPUT: There will be 5 sets of data. Each set contains two positive integers: N and P. N will be less than 10^{15} , and P will be valid. No input will cause an output to have a leading digit of 0.

OUTPUT: The transformed value of each input set. The printed number may not have any spaces between the digits.

SAMPLE INPUT: (http://www.datafiles.acsl.org/2020/contest1/int-sample-input.txt)

```
296351  5
762184  3
45873216  7
19750418  6
386257914  5
```

SAMPLE OUTPUT:

1. 193648
2. 873173
3. 95322341
4. 86727361
5. 831752441

AMERICAN COMPUTER SCIENCE LEAGUE

2019-2020 **Contest #1**

Intermediate Division - Number Transformation

TEST DATA

TEST INPUT:

```
4318672 4
35197545 1
975318642 9
9876543210 5
314159265358 10
```

TEST OUTPUT:

1. 2198216
2. 80642095
3. 924681357
4. 3210941234
5. 754315221114

American Computer Science League

2019-2020 — **Contest #1**

JUNIOR DIVISION

1. Computer Number Systems

Convert the date of this year's All-Star Contest: 5/23/2020 to hex. Write in the form: M/DD/YYY

1.

2. Computer Number Systems

Which number has the most 2's when converted to octal?

508_{16} $88A_{16}$ 195_{16} $348A_{16}$ 1050_{16}

2.

3. Recursive Functions

Find f(90) given:

$$f(x)=\begin{cases} 2 * f(x/3) - 1 & \text{if x is a multiple of 3 and odd} \\ -1 * f(x/2) + 2 & \text{if x is even} \\ x + 4 & \text{otherwise} \end{cases}$$

3.

4. Recursive Functions

Find f(f(f(6))) given:

$$f(x)=\begin{cases} 2 * f(x-3) - 1 & \text{if } x > 10 \\ f(x-2) + 3 & \text{if } 2 <= x <= 10 \\ 3\text{^}x * x\text{^}3 & \text{if } x < 2 \end{cases}$$

4.

American Computer Science League

2019-2020 — **Contest #1**

JUNIOR DIVISION

5. What Does This Program Do? - Branching

5.

What is outputted when this program is executed?

```
a = 12 : b = 6 : c = 3 : d = 2
if a  ==  b * d then
    e = a / b
end if
if b - d  ==  a / c then
    e = e + a / c
end if
e = a / c - e
if b / c ==  a / e then
    a = 2 * d
else
    a = 2 * e
end if
if (a < b) || (c < d) then
    a = a + b
else
    c = c + d
end if
if (a < d)  && (b + c > c * c) then
    d = a + c
else
    c = d - b
end if
x = b / a + c * e / (d + b) - (b + d) / a * a
print x
end
```

American Computer Science League

2019-2020 **Contest #1**

JUNIOR DIVISION SOLUTIONS

1. Computer Number Systems Convert each part to a hexadecimal number: M: 5 = 5_{16} DD: 23 = 17_{16} YYY: 2020 = $7E4_{16}$	**1.** 5/17/7E4 or 5_{16} / 17_{16} / $7E4_{16}$
2. Computer Number Systems 508_{16} = 10100001000_2 = 2410_8 $88A_{16}$ = 100010001010_2 = 4212_8 195_{16} = 110010101_2 = 625_8 $348A_{16}$ = 11010010001010_2 = 32212_8 1050_{16} = 1000001010000_2 = 10120_8	**2.** $348A_8$ or $348A$
3. Recursive Functions f(90) = -1 * f(90/2) + 2 = -1 * f(45) + 2 = -1 * 33 + 2 = -31 f(45) = 2 * f(45/3) - 1 = 2 * f(15) - 1 = 2 * 17 - 1 = 33 f(15) = 2 * f(15/3) - 1 = 2 * f(5) - 1 = 2 * 9 - 1 = 17 f(5) = 5 + 4 = 9	**3.** -31

American Computer Science League

2019-2020 Contest #1

JUNIOR DIVISION SOLUTIONS

4. Recursive Functions

f(6) = f(6-2) + 3 = f(4) + 3 = 6 + 3 = 9
f(4) = f(4-2) + 3 = f(2) + 3 = 3 + 3 = 6
f(2) = f(2-2) + 3 = f(0) + 3 = 0 + 3 = 3
f(0) = 3^0 * 0^3 = 0
f(9) = f(9-2) + 3 = f(7) + 3 = 12 + 3 = 15
f(7) = f(7-2) + 3 = f(5) + 3 = 9 + 3 = 12
f(5) = f(5-2) + 3 = f(3) + 3 = 6 + 3 = 9
f(3) = f(3-1) + 3 = f(1) + 3 = 3 + 3 = 6
f(1) = 3^1 * 1^3 = 3 * 1 = 3
f(15) = 2 * f(15-3) - 1 = 2 * f(12) - 1 = 2 * 29 - 1 = 57
f(12) = 2 * f(12-3) - 1 = 2 * f(9) - 1 = 2 * 15 - 1 =29
So f(f(f(6))) = f(f(9)) = f(15) = 57

4. 57

5. What Does This Program Do? - Branching

a	b	c	d	e
12	6	3	2	2
12	6	3	2	6
12	6	3	2	-2
-4	6	3	2	-2
2	6	3	2	-2
2	6	-4	2	-2

x = b / a + c * e / (d + b) - (b + d) / a * a
= 6 / 2 + (-4) * (-2) / (2 + 6) - (6 + 2) / 2 * 2
= 3 + 8 / 8 - 8 / 2 * 2
= 3 + 1 - 4 * 2 = 3 + 1 - 8 = -4

5. -4

AMERICAN COMPUTER SCIENCE LEAGUE

2019-2020 **Contest #1**

Junior Division - Number Transformation

PROBLEM: Given a positive integer (call it *N*), a position in that integer (call it *P*), and a transition integer (call it *D*). Transform *N* as follows:

- If the Pth digit of *N* from the right is from 0 to 4, add *D* to it. Replace the Pth digit by the units digit of the sum. Then, replace all digits to the right of the Pth digit by 0.

- If the Pth digit of *N* from the right is from 5 to 9, subtract *D* from it. Replace the Pth digit by the leftmost digit of the absolute value of the difference. Then, replace all digits to the right of the Pth digit by 0.

Example 1: $N = 7145032,\ P = 2,\ D = 8$. The 2nd digit from the right is 3; add 8 to it (3+8=11), and replace the 3 with 1 to get 7145012. Replace the digits to the right by 0s to get 7145010.

Example 2: $N = 1540670,\ P = 3,\ D = 54$. The 3rd digit from the right is 6; the absolute value of 6-54 is 48; replace with the 4 to get 1540470. Replace the digits to the right with 0s to get 1540400.

INPUT: There will be 5 sets of data. Each set contains 3 positive integers: *N, P*, and *D. N* will be less than 10^{15}; *P* and *D* will be valid inputs. No input will cause an output to have a leading digit of 0.

OUTPUT: Print the transformed number. The printed number may not have any spaces between the digits.

SAMPLE INPUT: (http://www.datafiles.acsl.org/2020/contest1/jr-sample-input.txt)

```
124987 2 3
540670 3 9
7145042 2 8
124987 2 523
4386709 1 2
```

SAMPLE OUTPUT:

1. **124950**
2. **540300**
3. **7145020**
4. **124950**
5. **4386707**

AMERICAN COMPUTER SCIENCE LEAGUE

2019-2020 Contest #1

Junior Division - Number Transformation

TEST DATA

TEST INPUT:

```
4318762 4 3
72431685 1 7
123456789 7 8
9876543210 10 25
314159265358 8 428
```

TEST OUTPUT:

1. 4315000
2. 72431682
3. 121000000
4. 1000000000
5. 314140000000

American Computer Science League

2019-2020 Contest #1

ELEMENTARY DIVISION

1. Computer Number Systems What is the base10 equivalent for 1357_8?	1.
2. Computer Number Systems Which of the following is the largest number? 657_8 $1AD_{16}$ 430_{10}	2.
3. Computer Number Systems Evaluate: $3275_8 + 4653_8 - 657_8$ Express the answer in octal.	3.
4. Computer Number Systems How many binary numbers have more 1's than 0's in the range of numbers from 16 to 31 in base 10 inclusive?	4.
5. Computer Number Systems What is the sum of the decimal values of the red and the blue component for a color that is represented by the hexadecimal number $A85F1C_{16}$?	5.

American Computer Science League

2019-2020 — **Contest #1**

ELEMENTARY DIVISION SOLUTIONS

1. Computer Number Systems $1357_8 = 7 * 8^0 + 5 * 8^1 + 3 * 8^2 + 1 * 8^3$ so $8^3 = 64 * 8 = 512$. $3 * 64 = 192$. Therefore, $7 + 40 + 192 + 512 = \mathbf{751_{10}}$.	**1.** 751 or 751_{10}
2. Computer Number Systems Convert the first and the last numbers to hexadecimal: $657_8 = 110\ 101\ 111_2 = 1\ 1010\ 1111_2 = 1AF_{16}$ $430_{10} - 256 = 174 - 160 = 14$ so $430_{10} = 1AE_{16}$ $\mathbf{1AD_{16}}$ is smaller than both of these so 657_8 is the largest.	**2.** 657 or 657_8
3. Computer Number Systems $3275_8 + 4653_8 = 10150_8$ so $10150_8 - 657_8 = \mathbf{7271_8}$ because you must carry 8 in adding and borrow 8 in subtracting.	**3.** 7271 or 7271_8
4. Computer Number Systems Counting in binary starting with 16 yields 10000, 10001, 10010, 10011, 10100, 10101, 10110, 10111, 11000, 11001, 11010, 11011, 11100, 11101, 11110, 11111. **11** of these have more 1's than 0's.	**4.** 11
5. Computer Number Systems Each color for an RGB code uses 2 hexadecimal digits. The RED component is the first 2 digits and the BLUE component is the last 2 digits. Converting $A8_{16}$ to base $10 = 10 * 16 + 8 = 168$ and $1C_{16}$ to base $10 = 1 * 16 + 12 = 28$. $168 + 28 = \mathbf{196_{10}}$.	**5.** 196 or 196_{10}

American Computer Science League

2019-2020 — Contest #1

CLASSROOM DIVISION

---

1. Computer Number Systems

Convert the date of this year's All-Star Contest: 5/23/2020 to hex. Write in the form: M/DD/YYY

1.

---

2. Computer Number Systems

Which number has the most 2's when converted to octal?

508_{16} $\quad 88A_{16}$ $\quad 195_{16}$ $\quad 348A_{16}$ $\quad 1050_{16}$

2.

---

3. Recursive Functions

Find f(90) given:

$$f(x) = \begin{cases} 2 * f(x/3) - 1 & \text{if x is a multiple of 3 and odd} \\ -1 * f(x/2) + 2 & \text{if x is even} \\ x + 4 & \text{otherwise} \end{cases}$$

3.

---

4. Recursive Functions

Find f(f(f(6))) given:

$$f(x) = \begin{cases} 2 * f(x-3) - 1 & \text{if } x > 10 \\ f(x-2) + 3 & \text{if } 2 <= x <= 10 \\ 3\text{^}x * x\text{^}3 & \text{if } x < 2 \end{cases}$$

4.

American Computer Science League

2019-2020 — Contest #1

CLASSROOM DIVISION

5. What Does This Program Do? - Branching

What is outputted when this program is executed?

```
a = 12 : b = 6 : c = 3 : d = 2
if a  ==  b * d then
   e = a / b
end if
if b - d  ==  a / c then
   e = e + a / c
end if
e = a / c - e
if b / c ==  a / e then
   a = 2 * d
else
   a = 2 * e
end if
if (a < b) || (c < d) then
   a = a + b
else
   c = c + d
end if
if (a < d)  && (b + c > c * c) then
    d = a + c
else
    c = d - b
end if
x = b / a + c * e / (d + b) - (b + d) / a * a
print x
end
```

5.

American Computer Science League

2019-2020 — Contest #1

CLASSROOM DIVISION

6. Computer Number Systems Convert 2019_{10} to octal. Write the octal digits in ascending order. Convert this new octal to hex.	**6.**
7. Computer Number Systems Which of the following has the fewest number of 1's in its binary representation? a) 4765_8 b) ABE_{16} c) 8271_{10} d) 1011111011_2	**7.**
8. Recursive Functions Find f(f(f(f(-5)))) given: $f(x)=\begin{cases} f(x+3)-2 & \text{if } x < 4 \\ f(2x-1)+1 & \text{if } 4 <= x <= 6 \\ x-4 & \text{if } x > 6 \end{cases}$	**8.**
9. Recursive Functions Given: f(1) = 3 f(2) = 5 f(n) = 3 * f(n - 1) - f(n - 2) Find the smallest value of n such that f(n) > 200.	**9.**

American Computer Science League

2019-2020 — Contest #1

CLASSROOM DIVISION

10. What Does This Program Do?

What is outputted when this program is executed?

```
a = 20: b = 4: c = 10: d = 2
if a < b then
    e = b - a
else
    f = a + b
end if
if b + c < a * a then
    b = b + c
else
    d = 2 * c
end if
if c > b && a < d then
    f = b + e
else
    e = f - c
end if
if a + d < b - c || f < d + c then
    a = e
else
    b = f
end if
if a * a < e * e || f > d then
    b = d * d
else
    d = a * a
end if
if b - a  > d - a then
    a = b
else
    b = f
end if
x =  (f / (a + d) - f / (b * d) + (e + d)/(a * b))^((f - e)/d)
print x
end
```

10.

American Computer Science League

2019-2020 **Contest #1**

CLASSROOM DIVISION SOLUTIONS

1. Computer Number Systems Convert each part to a hexadecimal number: M: 5 = 5_{16} DD: 23 = 17_{16} YYY: 2020 = $7E4_{16}$	**1.** 5/17/7E4 or 5_{16} / 17_{16} / $7E4_{16}$
2. Computer Number Systems 508_{16} = 10100001000_2 = 2410_8 $88A_{16}$ = 100010001010_2 = 4212_8 195_{16} = 110010101_2 = 625_8 $348A_{16}$ = 11010010001010_2 = 32212_8 1050_{16} = 1000001010000_2 = 10120_8	**2.** $348A_8$ or $348A$
3. Recursive Functions f(90) = -1 * f(90/2) + 2 = -1 * f(45) + 2 = -1 * 33 + 2 = -31 f(45) = 2 * f(45/3) - 1 = 2 * f(15) - 1 = 2 * 17 - 1 = 33 f(15) = 2 * f(15/3) - 1 = 2 * f(5) - 1 = 2 * 9 - 1 = 17 f(5) = 5 + 4 = 9	**3.** -31

American Computer Science League

2019-2020 Contest #1

CLASSROOM DIVISION SOLUTIONS

4. Recursive Functions

f(6) = f(6-2) + 3 = f(4) + 3 = 6 + 3 = 9
f(4) = f(4-2) + 3 = f(2) + 3 = 3 + 3 = 6
f(2) = f(2-2) + 3 = f(0) + 3 = 0 + 3 = 3
f(0) = 3^0 * 0^3 = 0
f(9) = f(9-2) + 3 = f(7) + 3 = 12 + 3 = 15
f(7) = f(7-2) + 3 = f(5) + 3 = 9 + 3 = 12
f(5) = f(5-2) + 3 = f(3) + 3 = 6 + 3 = 9
f(3) = f(3-1) + 3 = f(1) + 3 = 3 + 3 = 6
f(1) = 3^1 * 1^3 = 3 * 1 = 3
f(15) = 2 * f(15-3) - 1 = 2 * f(12) - 1 = 2 * 29 - 1 = 57
f(12) = 2 * f(12-3) - 1 = 2 * f(9) - 1 = 2 * 15 - 1 =29
So f(f(f(6))) = f(f(9)) = f(15) = 57

4. 57

5. What Does This Program Do? - Branching

a	b	c	d	e
12	6	3	2	2
12	6	3	2	6
12	6	3	2	-2
-4	6	3	2	-2
2	6	3	2	-2
2	6	-4	2	-2

x = b / a + c * e / (d + b) - (b + d) / a * a
  = 6 / 2 + (-4) * (-2) / (2 + 6) - (6 + 2) / 2 * 2
  = 3 + 8 / 8 - 8 / 2 * 2
  = 3 + 1 - 4 * 2 = 3 + 1 - 8 = -4

5. -4

American Computer Science League

2019-2020 — **Contest #1**

CLASSROOM DIVISION SOLUTIONS

---

6. Computer Number Systems

$2019_{10} = 3743_8$

Written in ascending octal digits: 3347_8

$3347_8 = 11\ 011\ 100\ 111_8$

$= 110\ 1110\ 0111_{16}$

$= 6 \quad E \quad 7_{16}$

6. $6E7_{16}$ or 6E7

---

7. Computer Number Systems

Convert each to binary:

a) $4765_8 = 100111110101_2$ — 8 1's

b) $ABE_{16} = 101010111110_2$ — 8 1's

c) $8271_{10} = 10000001001111_2$ — 6 1's

d) 1011111011_2 — 8 1's

7. 8271_{10} or 8271

---

8. Recursive Functions

f(-5) = f(-5 + 3) - 2 = f(-2) - 2 = 0 - 2 = -2
f(-2) = f(-2 + 3) - 2 = f(1) - 2 = 2 - 2 = 0
f(1) = f(1 + 3) - 2 = f(4) - 2 = 4 - 2 = 2
f(4) = f(2*4-1) + 1 = f(7) + 1 = 3 + 1 = 4
f(7) = 7 - 4 = 3
f(0) = f(0 + 3) - 2 = f(3) - 2 = 6 - 2 = 4
f(3) = f(3 + 3) - 2 = f(6) - 2 = 8 - 2 = 6
f(6) = f(2*6 - 1) + 1 = f(11) + 1 = 7 + 1 = 8
f(11) = 11 - 4 = 7
So f(f(f(f(-5)))) = f(f(f(-2)))
= f(f(0))
= f(4)
= 4

8. 4

American Computer Science League

2019-2020 Contest #1

CLASSROOM DIVISION SOLUTIONS

9. Recursive Functions

f(1) = 3
f(2) = 5
f(3) = 3 * f(2) - f(1) = 3 * 5 - 3 = 12
f(4) = 3 * f(3) - f(2) = 3 * 12 - 5 = 31
f(5) = 3 * f(4) - f(3) = 3 * 31 - 12 = 81
f(6) = 3 * f(5) - f(4) = 3 * 81 - 31 = 212 > 200

9. 6

10. What Does This Program Do?

a	b	c	d	e	f
20	4	10	2		
20	4	10	2		24
20	14	10	2		24
20	14	10	2	14	24
20	24	10	2	14	24
20	4	10	2	14	24
4	4	10	2	14	24

x = (f / (a + d) - f / (b * d) + (e + d)/(a * b))^((f - e)/d)
= (24/(4 + 2) - 24 /(4 * 2) + (14 + 2)/(4 * 4))^((24 - 14)/2)
= (24/6 - 24/8 + 16/16)^(10/2)
= (4 - 3 + 1)^5
= 2^5 = 32

10. 32

Contest #2

American Computer Science League

2019-2020 —— Contest #2

SENIOR DIVISION

1. Prefix/Infix/Postfix Notation Convert this prefix expression to postfix: $* \; a + a \uparrow + \uparrow a \, 2 * 4 \uparrow b \, 2 / 1 \, 2$	1.
2. Prefix/Infix/Postfix Notation Evaluate the following prefix expression if @abc = ½(a+b+c) and #abc = ⅓ (a*b*c): Note: all numbers are single digits. - # / + 7 5 2 - 6 * 4 1 ↑ 4 2 @ - 6 3 + 5 2 ↑ 2 3	2.
3. Bit-String Flicking Evaluate the following: (LCIRC-2 01101) OR (NOT 10110) AND (RSHIFT-1 (RCIRC-2 10110))	3.
4. Bit-String Flicking Solve for X (5 bit string): (LSHIFT -1 10111) OR (LCIRC -2 (RSHIFT - 1 X)) AND (RCIRC -3 (NOT 01101)) = 01110	4.
5. LISP Evaluate this LISP expression: (CAR (CDR (CAR (REVERSE (CDR ‘((a (b c)) c d (e (d a (c b (e)))))))))	5.

American Computer Science League

2019-2020 **Contest #2**

SENIOR DIVISION SOLUTIONS

1. Prefix/Infix/Postfix Notation Prefix: $* \; a + a \uparrow + \uparrow a\, 2 * 4 \uparrow b\, 2\, /\, 1\, 2$ $= * \; a + a \uparrow + (\uparrow a\, 2) * 4\, (\uparrow b\, 2)\, (/\, 1\, 2)$ $= * \; a + a \uparrow + (a \uparrow 2)\, (4 * (b \uparrow 2)\, (1/2)$ $= * \; a + a \uparrow ((a \uparrow 2) + (4 * (b \uparrow 2))\, (1/2)$ $= * \; a + a\, (((a \uparrow 2) + (4 * (b \uparrow 2)) \uparrow (1/2))$ $= * \; a\, (a + (((a \uparrow 2) + (4 * (b \uparrow 2)) \uparrow (1/2)))$ $= (a * (a + (((a \uparrow 2) + (4 * (b \uparrow 2)) \uparrow (1/2))))$ Infix: $a * (a + (a \uparrow 2 + 4 * b \uparrow 2) \uparrow (1/2))$ $= a * (a + ((a \uparrow 2) + 4 * (b \uparrow 2)) \uparrow (1\, 2\, /))$ $= a * (a + ((a\, 2 \uparrow) + (4 * (b\, 2 \uparrow))\, (\uparrow (1\, 2\, /)))$ $= a * (a + (a\, 2 \uparrow 4\, b\, 2 \uparrow * + 1\, 2\, / \uparrow))$ $= a * (a\; a\, 2 \uparrow 4\, b\, 2 \uparrow * + 1\, 2\, / \uparrow +)$ $= a\; a\; a\, 2 \uparrow 4\, b\, 2 \uparrow * + 1\, 2\, / \uparrow + *$ Postfix: $a\; a\; a\, 2 \uparrow 4\, b\, 2 \uparrow * + 1\, 2\, / \uparrow + *$ This is the formula for the surface area of a square pyramid with a base of length a and height of b.	**1.** As shown
2. Prefix/Infix/Postfix Notation - # / + 7 5 2 - 6 * 4 1 ↑ 4 2 @ - 6 3 + 5 2 ↑ 2 3 = - # / (+ 7 5) 2 - 6 (* 4 1) (↑ 4 2) @ (- 6 3) (+ 5 2) (↑ 2 3) = - # (/ 12 2) (- 6 4) 16 (@ 3 7 8) = - (# 6 2 16) 9 = (- 64 9) = 55	**2.** 55
3. Bit-String Flicking (LCIRC-2 01101) OR (NOT 10110) AND (RSHIFT-1 (RCIRC-2 10110)) = 10101 OR 01001 AND (RSHIFT-1 10101) = 10101 OR 01001 AND 01010 = 10101 OR 01000 = 11101	**3.** 11101

American Computer Science League

2019-2020 Contest #2

SENIOR DIVISION SOLUTIONS

4. Bit-String Flicking Let X = abcde LHS = (LSHIFT -1 10111) OR (LCIRC -2 (RSHIFT - 1 abcde)) AND RCIRC -3 (NOT 01101)) = 01110 OR (LCIRC -2 0abcd) AND (RCIRC -3 10010) = 01110 OR bcd0a AND 01010 = 01110 OR 0c000 = 01110 LHS = RHS = 01110 Therefore a = *, b = *, c =*, d = *, e = *	**4.** *****
5. LISP (CAR (CDR(CAR (REVERSE (CDR '((a (b c)) c d (e (d a (c b (e))))))))) = (CAR (CDR (CAR (REVERSE ' (c d (e (d a (c b (e)))))))) = (CAR (CDR (CAR ' ((e (d a (c b (e))))d c)))) = (CAR (CDR ' (e (d a (c b (e)))))) = (CAR ' ((d a (c b (e))))) = (d a (c b (e)))	**5.** (d a (c b (e)))

2019-2020 **AMERICAN COMPUTER SCIENCE LEAGUE** Contest #2

Senior Division - ACSL Difference Factor

PROBLEM: Given 2 strings, calculate the ACSL Difference Factor (ADF). The rules are:

- Ignore all non-alphabetic characters and convert all letters to uppercase.
- Find the longest common substring contained in the two strings. If there is more than one longest substring, use the one that is alphabetically first. If the same longest substring occurs more than once in a string, use the leftmost occurrence.
- Remove that substring from both strings.
- Separate each string into two parts, one to the left and the other to the right of the now deleted common substring.
- Take the left part of both strings and repeat the process to find and delete the longest common substring. Do the same to the right part of both strings.
- Repeat the process above until no new pair contains a common substring.
- The ADF is the sum of the lengths of all of the longest common substrings found.

Example:

<table>
<tr><td colspan="4">(I AM GOING HOME NOW) (I WILL GO HOME SOON)</td></tr>
<tr><td colspan="2">(I AM GOING) (I WILL GO) |</td><td colspan="2">(NOW) (SOON)</td></tr>
<tr><td>(I AM) (I WILL) |</td><td>(ING) ( ) |</td><td>( ) (SOO) |</td><td>(OW) ( )</td></tr>
<tr><td colspan="4">( ) ( ) | (AM) (WILL) |</td></tr>
</table>

The common substrings are: *HOME, GO, I,* and *N.* The ADF = 4 + 2 + 1 + 1 = 8.

INPUT: There will be 5 inputs. Each input contains 2 strings separated by a carriage return, each fewer than 200 characters. Blank lines in the Sample Input are for illustration only and not in the actual file.

OUTPUT: For each input, print the ADF as described above.

Senior Division - ACSL Difference Factor

SAMPLE INPUT: (http://www.datafiles.acsl.org/2020/contest2/sr-sample-input.txt)

```
I am going home now
I will go home now

The big black bear bit a big black bug
The big black bug bled black blood

Complementary angle measures sum to 90 degrees.
The measures of supplementary angles add to 180 degrees.

A Tale of Two Cities was published by Dickens in 1859.
In 1839, Charles Dickens published Nicholas Nickleby.

Connecticut is The Constitution State.
Hartford is the capital of Connecticut.
```

SAMPLE OUTPUT:

```
1. 10
2. 19
3. 26
4. 18
5. 11
```

Senior Division - ACSL Difference Factor

TEST DATA

TEST INPUT:

```
To be or not to be, that is the question.
To err is human; to really foul things up requires a computer.

The Pythagorean Theorem says that the sum of the squares of
the two legs equals the square of the hypotenuse.
To find a leg using the Pythagorean Theorem, take the square
root of the hypotenuse squared minus the other leg squared.

Uncle Tom's Cabin was published by Harriet Beecher Stowe in
1852.
In 1876, Mark Twain published The Adventures of Tom Sawyer.

Once upon a midnight dreary while I pondered weak and weary,
Over many a quaint and curious volume of forgotten lore.

A tutor who tooted the flute tried to tutor two tooters to
toot!
Is it harder to toot or to tutor two tooters to toot?
```

TEST OUTPUT:

```
1. 14
2. 50
3. 20
4. 9
5. 31
```

American Computer Science League

2019-2020 — Contest #2

INTERMEDIATE DIVISION

1. Prefix/Infix/Postfix Notation Convert the following infix expression to a postfix expression: $\frac{A+B^2}{A^2} - \frac{AC}{B} + ABC$	**1.**
2. Prefix/Infix/Postfix Notation Evaluate this prefix expression: (Note: all numbers are single digits) + − ∗ 4 − 8 / 6 3 / + ↑ 3 2 ↑ 4 2 5 / / ↑ 6 3 * 4 3 2	**2.**
3. Bit-String Flicking Evaluate the following 6-bit expression: (LSHIFT-1 (LCIRC-2 (RSHIFT-1 (NOT 100001))))	**3.**
4. Bit-String Flicking Solve for X (5 - bit string): (LCIRC-2 (RCIRC-4 X OR LSHIFT-1 01001 AND NOT 01010)) = 10011	**4.**
5. LISP Evaluate the following LISP expression: (CAR (CDR (CAR (CDR ‘(1 (2 (3 4)(5 6) 7) 8)))))	**5.**

American Computer Science League

2019-2020 — **Contest #2**

INTERMEDIATE DIVISION SOLUTIONS

1. Prefix/Infix/Postfix Notation

$$\frac{A+B^2}{A^2}-\frac{AC}{B}+ABC$$

= ((A + B ↑ 2) / (A ↑ 2)) - ((A * C) / B) + (A * B * C)
= ((A + (B 2 ↑)) / (A 2 ↑)) - (A C * B /) + (A B * C *)
= (A B 2 ↑ + A 2 ↑ /) - (A C * B /) + (A B * C * +)
= A B 2 ↑ + A 2 ↑ / A C * B / - A B * C * +

1. As shown

2. Prefix/Infix/Postfix Notation

\+ − ∗ 4 − 8 / 6 3 / + ↑ 3 2 ↑ 4 2 5 / / ↑ 6 3 * 4 3 2
= + − ∗ 4 − 8 (/ 6 3) / + (↑ 3 2) (↑ 4 2) 5 / / (↑ 6 3) (* 4 3) 2
= + − ∗ 4 (− 8 2) / (+9 16) 5 / (/ 216 12) 2
= + − (∗ 4 6) (/ 25 5) (/ 18 2)
= +(− 24 5) 9
= + 19 9
= 28

2. 28

3. Bit-String Flicking

(LSHIFT-1 (LCIRC-2 (RSHIFT-1 (NOT 100001))))
= (LSHIFT-1 (LCIRC-2 (RSHIFT-1 011110)))
= (LSHIFT-1 (LCIRC-2 001111))
= (LSHIFT-1 111100)
= 111000

3. 111000

American Computer Science League

2019-2020 Contest #2

INTERMEDIATE DIVISION SOLUTIONS

4. Bit-String Flicking Let X = abcde LHS = (LCIRC-2 (RCIRC-4 X OR LSHIFT-1 01001 AND NOT 01010)) = (LCIRC-2 (RCIRC-4 abcde OR LSHIFT-1 01001 AND NOT 01010)) = (LCIRC-2 (bcdea OR 10010 AND 10101)) = (LCIRC-2 (bcdea OR 10000)) = (LCIRC-2 1cdea) = dea1c So dea1c = 10011. Then d = 1, e = 0, a = 0, c = 1, b = * → 0*110	**4.** 0*110
5. LISP (CAR (CDR (CAR (CDR '(1 (2 (3 4)(5 6) 7) 8))))) = (CAR (CDR (CAR '((2 (3 4)(5 6) 7) 8)))) = (CAR (CDR '(2 (3 4)(5 6) 7))) = (CAR '((3 4)(5 6) 7)) = (3 4)	**5.** (3 4)

2019-2020

ACSL

AMERICAN COMPUTER SCIENCE LEAGUE

Contest #2

Intermediate Division - ACSL Sameness Factor

PROBLEM: Given 2 strings, separated by a space, calculate the ACSL Sameness Factor (ASF). Repeat the following 3 steps in order until no other deleting aligns like characters:

- Align the strings from left to right.
- Delete the like characters in the like locations from left to right.
- Proceeding from left to right, if the like location characters are not the same and deleting a character at a location in one of the strings which shifts the remaining characters to the left causes like characters to be at that location, delete those characters and any other like characters at like locations. If there is a case as in NAPE and ANTI where it is possible to delete a character at the same location in both strings, then delete it in the second string. Therefore, the A would be deleted and the NTI shifted to the left.

Calculate the ACSL Sameness Factor by doing the following:

- Calculate the difference in the alphabetic locations from the aligned string characters in the second string to the string character in the first string. B to D would add 2 to the ASF. D to B would add -2 to the ASF.
- If there are characters remaining in one of the strings, add the number of those characters to the ASF.

Example: ABCDEFT ABXCGBTZFP

ABCDEFT → ~~AB~~CDEF~~T~~ → CDEF → ~~C~~DEF → DEF → DE~~F~~ → DE
ABXCGBTZFP → ~~AB~~XCGB~~T~~ZFP → ~~X~~CGBZFP → ~~C~~GBZFP → GB~~Z~~FP → GB~~F~~P → GBP

The ASF is calculated as: G to D = -3 B to E = + 3 P = + 1 (-3 + 3 + 1 = 1)

INPUT: There will be 5 inputs. Each input will contain 2 strings separated by a space and each fewer than 200 characters.

OUTPUT: For each input, print the ASF as described above.

SAMPLE INPUT **SAMPLE OUTPUT:**
(http://www.datafiles.acsl.org/2020/contest2/int-sample-input.txt)

```
BLAMEABLENESSES BLAMELESSNESSES        1.  -35
MEZZAMINES RAZZMATAZZ                  2.  -5
ABBREVIATIONS ABBREVIATORS             3.  -4
ABCDEFGHIJKLMNO ABKCLDZZHQJWWLX        4.  -86
ABCDEFGHIJKL ABXEWFRRH                 5.  -52
```

Intermediate Division - ACSL Sameness Factor

TEST DATA

TEST INPUT:

```
MYARTLOLLIPOPS MYLARBALLOONS
MASSACHUSETTSBAYCOLONY MINUTEMANNATIONALHISTORICALPARK
LOWERMACTOWNSHIPPA CRANBERRYTOWNSHIPPA
AMERICANCOMPUTERSCIENCELEAGUE NATIONALACADEMICGAMESLEAGUE
ABCDEFGHIJK ABDCEFGKILKJMN
```

TEST OUTPUT:

```
1. 23
2. 27
3. 11
4. 68
5. -9
```

American Computer Science League

2019-2020 — Contest #2

JUNIOR DIVISION

1. Prefix/Infix/Postfix Notation Convert this infix expression to a postfix expression: a + b * c - 2 * (a * b - c) / (a ^ 2 - b ^ 2)	**1.**
2. Prefix/Infix/Postfix Notation Evaluate this prefix expression: (Note: all numbers are single digits) + - / + 8 ^ 4 2 ^ 2 2 / * 3 2 6 / * / 8 4 2 4	**2.**
3. Bit-String Flicking Evaluate the following expression: 10110 OR 11001 AND 01011	**3.**
4. Bit-String Flicking Evaluate the following expression: (RSHIFT-1 (LCIRC-2 (LSHIFT-3 (RCIRC-2 10101))))	**4.**

American Computer Science League

2019-2020 Contest #2

JUNIOR DIVISION

5. What Does This Program Do? - Loops | 5.

Which of the following inputs would be printed by the program below?
5, 7, 15, 31, 35, 63, 101, 127, 255, 1023

```
INPUT N
FOR B = 3 TO N - 1 STEP 2
      IF N / B == INT(N / B) THEN
          END
      END IF
 NEXT B
FOR I = 1 TO 20
      IF N == 2 ^ I - 1 THEN
          PRINT N
      END IF
NEXT I
END
```

American Computer Science League

2019-2020 **Contest #2**

JUNIOR DIVISION SOLUTIONS

1. Prefix/Infix/Postfix Notation a + b * c - 2 * (a * b - c) / (a ^ 2 - b ^ 2) = a + (b * c) - 2 * ((a * b) - c) / ((a ^ 2) - (b ^ 2)) = a + (b c *) - 2 * ((a b *) - c) / ((a 2 ^) - (b 2 ^)) = a + (b c *) - 2 * (a b * c -) / (a 2 ^ b 2 ^ -) = a + (b c *) - (2 a b * c - *) / (a 2 ^ b 2 ^ -) = a + (b c *) - (2 a b * c - * a 2 ^ b 2 ^ - /) = a b c * + 2 a b * c - * a 2 ^ b 2 ^ - / -	**1.** As shown
2. Prefix/Infix/Postfix Notation + - / + 8 ^ 4 2 ^ 2 2 / * 3 2 6 / * / 8 4 2 4 = + - / + 8 (^ 4 2)(^ 2 2) / (* 3 2) 6 / * (/ 8 4) 2 4 = + - / + 8 (4 ^ 2)(2 ^ 2) / (3 * 2) 6 / * (8 / 4) 2 4 = + - / (+ 8 16) 4 (/ 6 6) / (* 2 2) 4 = + - / (8 + 16) 4 (6 / 6) / (2 * 2) 4 = + - (/ 24 4) 1 (/ 4 4) = + - (24 / 4) 1 (4 / 4) = + (- 6 1) 1 = + (6 - 1) 1 = (+ 5 1) = (5 + 1) = 6	**2.** 6
3. Bit-String Flicking 10110 OR 11001 AND 01011 = 10110 OR (11001 AND 01011) = 10110 OR 01001 = 11111	**3.** 11111

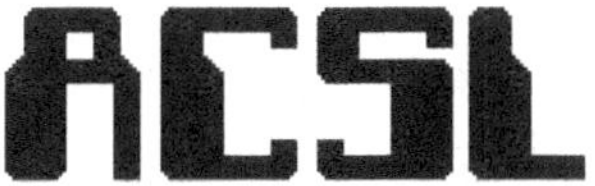

American Computer Science League

2019-2020 — **Contest #2**

JUNIOR DIVISION SOLUTIONS

4. Bit-String Flicking (RSHIFT-1 (LCIRC-2 (LSHIFT-3 (RCIRC-2 10101)))) = (RSHIFT-1 (LCIRC-2 (LSHIFT-3 01101))) = (RSHIFT-1 (LCIRC-2 01000)) = (RSHIFT-1 00001) = 00000	**4.** 00000
5. What Does This Program Do? - Loops A Mersenne Prime is a prime number that is one less than a power of 2. This program first checks to see if the inputted number is prime (B loop). They are: 5, 7, 31, 101, and 127. If it is, it then checks to see if it is one less than a power of 2. (I loop). There are 3: 7, 31, and 127.	**5.** 7, 31, 127

Junior Division - ACSL String Differences

PROBLEM: Given 2 strings with all capital letters, eliminate characters using each of the rules below once until only different characters align. The rules are performed in the following order:

- Delete the second occurance of any double consonant. There will not be more than 2 of the same consonant together.
- Delete all vowels (A, E, I, O, U) unless the vowel is the first character in the string.
- Align the resulting strings from left to right. Then delete all like characters at like positions.
- Align the remaining characters from right to left. Then delete like characters at like positions starting from the end of the string.

Example: MISSISSIPPI
MISSOURI

After removing the double consonants:	MISISIPI MISOURI
After removing the vowels:	MSSP MSR
After removing letters from L to R in same location:	SP R
After removing letters from R to L in the same location (no changes):	SP R

Output: R

INPUT: There will be 5 inputs. Each input will contain 2 strings separated by a single space and each fewer than 80 characters.

OUTPUT: For each input, print the shorter of the two resulting strings or the first in alphabetical order if they have the same length. We guarantee that neither is an empty string.

SAMPLE INPUT **SAMPLE OUTPUT:**
http://www.datafiles.acsl.org/2020/contest2/jr-sample-input.txt

MISSISSIPPI MISSOURI	1. R
CATHERINE KATHERYNE	2. C
CONSTITUTIONAL CONVENTIONAL	3. VN
COMPARTMENTALIZATION SEMIAUTOBIOGRAPHICAL	4. SBGRPHCL
PHYSICIAN PHARMACY	5. RMY

Junior Division - ACSL String Differences

TEST DATA

TEST INPUT:

```
FEEFIFOFUM FIDDLEDEEDEE
MYLOLLIPOPS MYLARBALLOONS
CONNECTICUTCT CONSTITUTIONSTATE
MASSACHUSETTSBAYCOLONY MINUTEMANNATIONALHISTORICALPARK
AMERICANCOMPUTERSCIENCELEAGUE NATIONALACADEMICGAMESLEAGUE
```

TEST OUTPUT:

1. DLDD
2. LPP
3. CCC
4. SCSBYCLNY
5. NTNLCDGM

American Computer Science League

2019-2020 **Contest #2**

ELEMENTARY DIVISION

1. Prefix / Infix / Postfix Evaluate the following prefix expression: (Note: all numbers are single digits) / − + * 7 3 * 2 5 ^ 3 2 2	**1.**
2. Prefix / Infix / Postfix Evaluate the following postfix expression: (Note: all numbers are single digits) 9 1 − 8 4 + 2 3 * / ^ 7 3 1 − ^ −	**2.**
3. Prefix / Infix / Postfix Convert the following infix expression to postfix: $\frac{6 + 3 * 7 - 8}{5^2 - 6}$	**3.**
4. Prefix / Infix / Postfix Convert the following infix expression to prefix: (7 − 1) * (5 + 2) / (3 ^ 2 − 7)	**4.**
5. Prefix / Infix / Postfix Convert the following prefix expression to postfix: / * / + 8 4 − 5 1 ^ 5 2 / + 7 2 3	**5.**

American Computer Science League

2019-2020 —— Contest #2

ELEMENTARY DIVISION SOLUTIONS

1. Prefix / Infix / Postfix / − + * 7 3 * 2 5 ^ 3 2 2 = / − + (7 * 3) (2 * 5) (3 ^ 2) 2 = / − (21 + 10) 9 2 = / (31 − 9) 2 = 22 / 2 = **11**	**1.** 11
2. Prefix / Infix / Postfix 9 1 − 8 4 + 2 3 * / ^ 7 3 1 − ^ − = ((9 − 1) ((8 + 4) (2 * 3) /) ^) (7 (3 − 1) ^) − = (8 (12 / 6) ^) (7 ^ 2) − = (8 ^ 2) − 49 = 64 − 49 = **15**	**2.** 15
3. Prefix / Infix / Postfix $\frac{6+3\cdot 7-8}{5^2-6}$ = (6 + (3 7 *) − 8) / ((5 2 ^) − 6) = (6 3 7 * + 8 −) / (5 2 ^ 6 −) = **6 3 7 * + 8 − 5 2 ^ 6 − /**	**3.** 6 3 7 * + 8 − 5 2 ^ 6 − /
4. Prefix / Infix / Postfix (7 − 1) * (5 + 2) / (3 ^ 2 − 7) = (− 7 1) * (+ 5 2) / ((^ 3 2) − 7) = (* − 7 1 + 5 2) / (− ^ 3 2 7) = **/ * − 7 1 + 5 2 − ^ 3 2 7**	**4.** / * − 7 1 + 5 2 − ^ 3 2 7
5. Prefix / Infix / Postfix / * / + 8 4 − 5 1 ^ 5 2 / + 7 2 3 = (/ (* (/ (+ 8 4) (− 5 1)) (^ 5 2)) (/ (+ 7 2) 3)) = (/ (* (/ (8 4 +) (5 1 −)) (5 2 ^)) (/ (7 2 +) 3)) = (/ (* (8 4 + 5 1 − /) (5 2 ^)) (7 2 + 3 /)) = / (8 4 + 5 1 − / 5 2 ^ *) (7 2 + 3 /) = **8 4 + 5 1 − / 5 2 ^ * 7 2 + 3 / /**	**5.** 8 4 + 5 1 − / 5 2 ^ * 7 2 + 3 / /

American Computer Science League

2019-2020 — **Contest #2**

CLASSROOM DIVISION

1. Prefix/Infix/Postfix Notation Convert this infix expression to a postfix expression: a + b * c - 2 * (a * b - c) / (a ^ 2 - b ^ 2)	**1.**
2. Prefix/Infix/Postfix Notation Evaluate this prefix expression: (Note: all numbers are single digits) + - / + 8 ^ 4 2 ^ 2 2 / * 3 2 6 / * / 8 4 2 4	**2.**
3. Bit-String Flicking Evaluate the following expression: 10110 OR 11001 AND 01011	**3.**
4. Bit-String Flicking Evaluate the following expression: (RSHIFT-1 (LCIRC-2 (LSHIFT-3 (RCIRC-2 10101))))	**4.**

American Computer Science League

2019-2020 Contest #2

CLASSROOM DIVISION

5. What Does This Program Do? - Loops

Which of the following inputs would be printed by the program below?
5, 7, 15, 31, 35, 63, 101, 127, 255, 1023

```
INPUT N
FOR B = 3 TO N - 1 STEP 2
      IF N / B == INT(N / B) THEN
          END
      END IF
NEXT B
FOR I = 1 TO 20
      IF N == 2 ^ I - 1 THEN
          PRINT N
      END IF
NEXT I
END
```

5.

American Computer Science League

2019-2020 — Contest #2

CLASSROOM DIVISION

6. Prefix/Infix/Postfix Notation Convert the following infix expression to a postfix expression: $\frac{A+B^2}{A^2} - \frac{AC}{B} + ABC$	**6.**
7. Prefix/Infix/Postfix Notation Evaluate this prefix expression: (Note: all numbers are single digits) + − * 4 − 8 / 6 3 / + ↑ 3 2 ↑ 4 2 5 / / ↑ 6 3 * 4 3 2	**7.**
8. Bit-String Flicking Evaluate the following 6-bit expression: (LSHIFT-1 (LCIRC-2 (RSHIFT-1 (NOT 100001))))	**8.**
9. Bit-String Flicking Solve for X (5 - bit string): (LCIRC-2 (RCIRC-4 X OR LSHIFT-1 01001 AND NOT 01010)) = 10011	**9.**
10. LISP Evaluate the following LISP expression: (CAR (CDR (CAR (CDR ‘(1 (2 (3 4)(5 6) 7) 8)))))	**10.**

American Computer Science League

2019-2020 — **Contest #2**

CLASSROOM DIVISION SOLUTIONS

1. Prefix/Infix/Postfix Notation a + b * c - 2 * (a * b - c) / (a ^ 2 - b ^ 2) = a + (b * c) - 2 * ((a * b) - c) / ((a ^ 2) - (b ^ 2)) = a + (b c *) - 2 * ((a b *) - c) / ((a 2 ^) - (b 2 ^)) = a + (b c *) - 2 * (a b * c -) / (a 2 ^ b 2 ^ -) = a + (b c *) - (2 a b * c - *) / (a 2 ^ b 2 ^ -) = a + (b c *) - (2 a b * c - * a 2 ^ b 2 ^ - /) = a b c * + 2 a b * c - * a 2 ^ b 2 ^ - / -	**1.** As shown
2. Prefix/Infix/Postfix Notation + - / + 8 ^ 4 2 ^ 2 2 / * 3 2 6 / * / 8 4 2 4 = + - / + 8 (^ 4 2)(^ 2 2) / (* 3 2) 6 / * (/ 8 4) 2 4 = + - / + 8 (4 ^ 2)(2 ^ 2) / (3 * 2) 6 / * (8 / 4) 2 4 = + - / (+ 8 16) 4 (/ 6 6) / (* 2 2) 4 = + - / (8 + 16) 4 (6 / 6) / (2 * 2) 4 = + - (/ 24 4) 1 (/ 4 4) = + - (24 / 4) 1 (4 / 4) = + (- 6 1) 1 = + (6 - 1) 1 = (+ 5 1) = (5 + 1) = 6	**2.** 6
3. Bit-String Flicking 10110 OR 11001 AND 01011 = 10110 OR (11001 AND 01011) = 10110 OR 01001 = 11111	**3.** 11111

American Computer Science League

2019-2020 — Contest #2

CLASSROOM DIVISION SOLUTIONS

4. Bit-String Flicking (RSHIFT-1 (LCIRC-2 (LSHIFT-3 (RCIRC-2 10101)))) = (RSHIFT-1 (LCIRC-2 (LSHIFT-3 01101))) = (RSHIFT-1 (LCIRC-2 01000)) = (RSHIFT-1 00001) = 00000	**4.** 00000
5. What Does This Program Do? - Loops A Mersenne Prime is a prime number that is one less than a power of 2. This program first checks to see if the inputted number is prime (B loop). They are: 5, 7, 31, 101, and 127. If it is, it then checks to see if it is one less than a power of 2. (I loop). There are 3: 7, 31, and 127.	**5.** 7, 31, 127

American Computer Science League

2019-2020 — **Contest #2**

CLASSROOM DIVISION SOLUTIONS

6. Prefix/Infix/Postfix Notation $\frac{A+B^2}{A^2} - \frac{AC}{B} + ABC$ = ((A + B ↑ 2) / (A ↑ 2)) - ((A * C) / B) + (A * B * C) = ((A + (B 2 ↑)) / (A 2 ↑)) - (A C * B /) + (A B * C *) = (A B 2 ↑ + A 2 ↑ /) - (A C * B /) + (A B * C * +) = A B 2 ↑ + A 2 ↑ / A C * B / - A B * C * +	**6** As shown
7. Prefix/Infix/Postfix Notation + − * 4 − 8 / 6 3 / + ↑ 3 2 ↑ 4 2 5 / / ↑ 6 3 * 4 3 2 = + − * 4 − 8 (/ 6 3) / + (↑ 3 2) (↑ 4 2) 5 / / (↑ 6 3) (* 4 3) 2 = + − * 4 (− 8 2) / (+ 9 16) 5 / (/ 216 12) 2 = + − (* 4 6) (/ 25 5) (/ 18 2) = + (− 24 5) 9 = + 19 9 = 28	**7.** 28
8. Bit-String Flicking (LSHIFT-1 (LCIRC-2 (RSHIFT-1 (NOT 100001)))) = (LSHIFT-1 (LCIRC-2 (RSHIFT-1 011110))) = (LSHIFT-1 (LCIRC-2 001111)) = (LSHIFT-1 111100) = 111000	**8.** 111000

ACSL

American Computer Science League

2019-2020 — Contest #2

CLASSROOM DIVISION SOLUTIONS

9. Bit-String Flicking Let X = abcde LHS = (LCIRC-2 (RCIRC-4 X OR LSHIFT-1 01001 AND NOT 01010)) = (LCIRC-2 (RCIRC-4 abcde OR LSHIFT-1 01001 AND NOT 01010)) = (LCIRC-2 (bcdea OR 10010 AND 10101)) = (LCIRC-2 (bcdea OR 10000)) = (LCIRC-2 1cdea) = dea1c So dea1c = 10011. Then d = 1, e = 0, a = 0, c = 1, b = * → 0*110	**9.** 0*110
10. LISP (CAR (CDR (CAR (CDR ‘(1 (2 (3 4)(5 6) 7) 8))))) = (CAR (CDR (CAR ‘((2 (3 4)(5 6) 7) 8)))) = (CAR (CDR ‘(2 (3 4)(5 6) 7))) = (CAR ‘((3 4)(5 6) 7)) = (3 4)	**10.** (3 4)

Contest #3

American Computer Science League

2019-2020 — **Contest #3**

SENIOR DIVISION

1. Boolean Algebra How many ordered triples make the following FALSE? $A\overline{B} + C(\overline{A} + B) + \overline{A}(B + \overline{C})$	**1.**
2. Boolean Algebra Which ordered triples make the following TRUE? $C(A \oplus \overline{B}) + B(A \oplus C) + \overline{A}(B \oplus \overline{C})$	**2.**
3. Data Structures What is the internal path length in the binary search tree for: ACADEMYOFAEROSPACEANDENGINEERING	**3.**
4. Data Structures Given an initially empty stack and the following commands on the stack, what will the next popped item be? PUSH(T), PUSH(H), PUSH(E), POP(X), PUSH(P), PUSH(H), POP(X), PUSH(A), PUSH(N), PUSH(T),POP(X), POP(X), POP(X), PUSH(O), PUSH(M), POP(X), POP(X), PUSH(O), PUSH(F), PUSH(T), PUSH(H), POP(X), POP(X), PUSH(E), PUSH(O), POP(X), PUSH(P), PUSH(E), PUSH(R), POP(X), POP(X), POP(X), PUSH(A), POP(X), POP(X).	**4.**

American Computer Science League

2019-2020 Contest #3

SENIOR DIVISION

5. FSA's and Regular Expressions

5.

Translate the following FSA into the Regular Expression it represents:

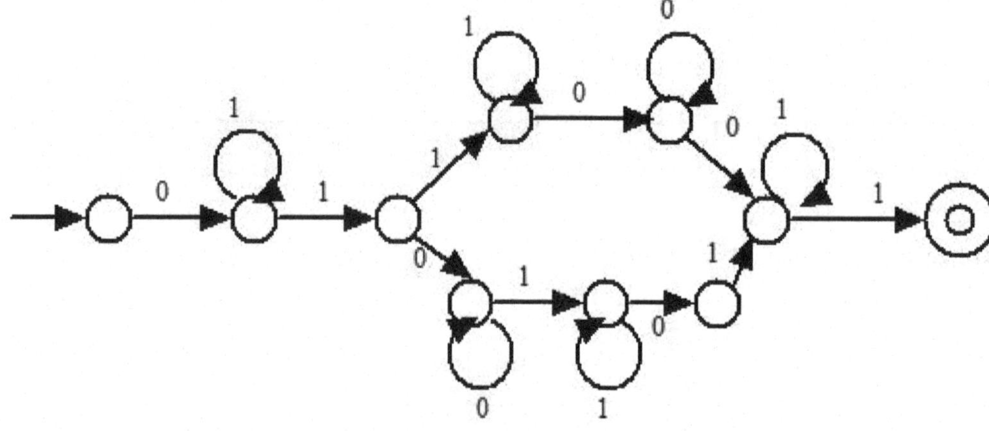

American Computer Science League

2019-2020 — **Contest #3**

SENIOR DIVISION SOLUTIONS

1. Boolean Algebra

$$A\overline{B} + C(\overline{A} + B) + \overline{A}(B + \overline{C})$$
$$= A\overline{B} + \overline{A}C + BC + \overline{A}B + \overline{A}\,\overline{C}$$
$$= \overline{A}(B + C + \overline{C}) + A\overline{B} + BC$$
$$= \overline{A} + A\overline{B} + BC$$
$$\overline{A} + A\overline{B} + BC = 0 \rightarrow \overline{A} = 0 \rightarrow A = 1$$
$$0 + 1\overline{B} + BC = 0 \rightarrow \overline{B} = 0 \rightarrow B = 1 \wedge C = 0 \Rightarrow (1, 1, 0)$$

1. 1

2. Boolean Algebra

$$C(A \oplus \overline{B}) + B(A \oplus C) + \overline{A}(B \oplus \overline{C})$$
$$= C(AB + \overline{A}\,\overline{B}) + B(A\overline{C} + \overline{A}C) + \overline{A}(BC + \overline{B}\,\overline{C})$$
$$= ABC + \overline{A}\,\overline{B}C + AB\overline{C} + \overline{A}BC + \overline{A}BC + \overline{A}\,\overline{B}\,\overline{C}$$
$$= BC(A + \overline{A}) + \overline{A}C(B + \overline{B}) + \overline{A}\,\overline{B}\,\overline{C}$$
$$= BC + \overline{A}C + \overline{A}\,\overline{B}\,\overline{C}$$
$$BC + \overline{A}C + \overline{A}\,\overline{B}\,\overline{C} = 1$$
$$C = 0 \rightarrow \overline{A}\,\overline{B} = 1 \rightarrow A = 0 \wedge B = 0 \Rightarrow (0, 0, 0)$$
$$C = 1 \rightarrow B + \overline{A} = 1 \Rightarrow (1, 1, 1), (0, 0, 1), (0, 1, 1)$$

2. (0, 0, 0)
(0, 0, 1)
(0, 1, 1)
(1, 1, 1)
(1, 1, 0)

American Computer Science League

2019-2020 Contest #3

SENIOR DIVISION SOLUTIONS

3. Data Structures

The binary search tree is:

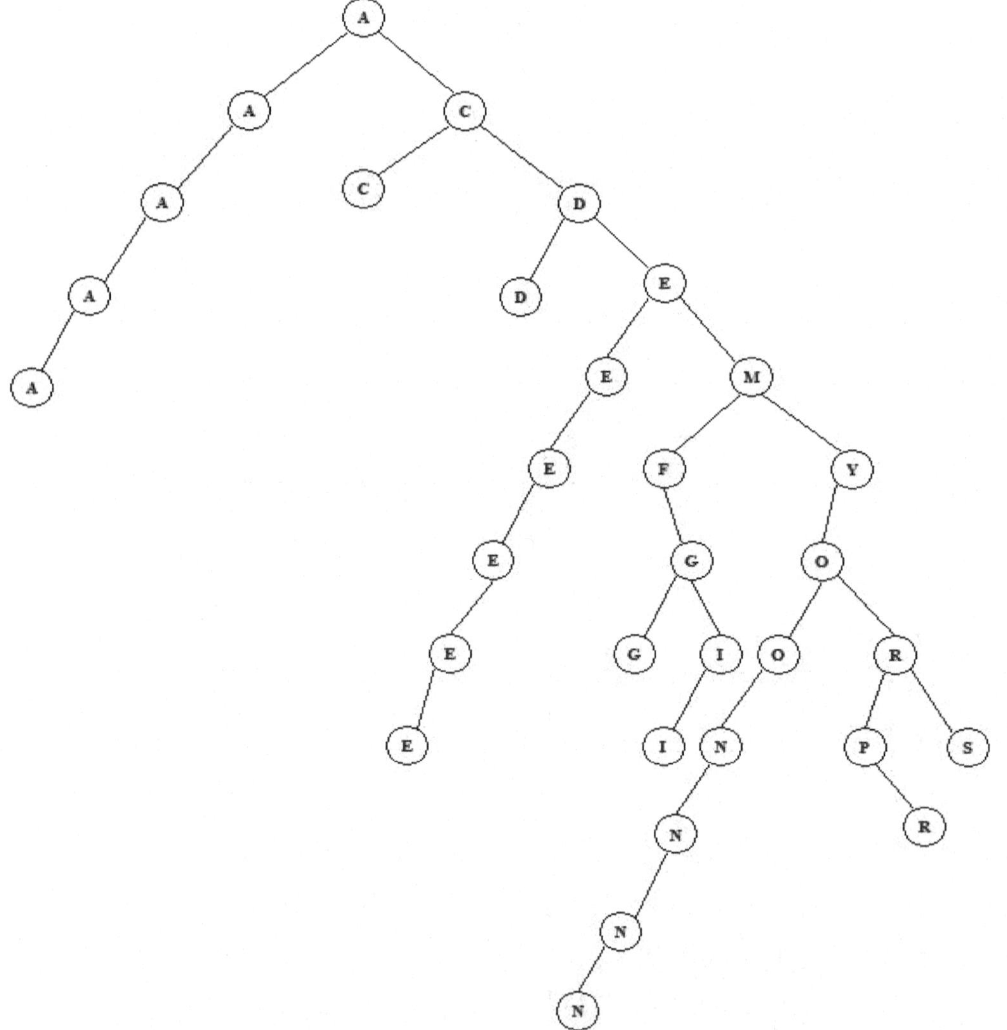

The internal path length is 2 * 1 + 3 * 2 + 3 * 3 + 3 * 4 + 3 * 5 + 3 * 6 + 5 * 7 + 5 * 8 + 2 * 9 + 1 * 10 + 1 * 11 = 2 + 6 + 9 + 12 + 15 + 18 + 35 + 40 + 18 + 10 + 11 = 176.

3. 176

American Computer Science League

2019-2020 — **Contest #3**

SENIOR DIVISION SOLUTIONS

4. Data Structures The stack is constructed using LIFO as follows: T, TH, THE, TH, THP, THPH, THP, THPA, THPAN, THPANT, THPAN, THPA, THP, THPO, THPOM, THPO, THP, THPO, THPOF, THPOFT, THPOFTH, THPOFT, THPOF, THPOFE, THPOFEO, THPOFE, THPOFEP, THPOFEPE, THPOFEPER, THPOFEPE, THPOFEP, THPOFE, THPOFEA, THPOFE, THPOF. The next item popped would be F.	**4.** F
5. FSA's and Regular Expressions The FSA translates to: 01*1(11*00*0 ∪ 00*11*01)1*1	**5.** As shown

2019-2020 **AMERICAN COMPUTER SCIENCE LEAGUE** Contest #3

Senior Division - Veitch

1

	A	A	~A	~A	
B			X	X	~D
B			X	X	D
~B			X	X	D
~B			X	X	~D
	~C	C	C	~C	

2

	A	A	~A	~A	
B					~D
B					D
~B	X	X			D
~B	X	X			~D
	~C	C	C	~C	

3

	A	A	~A	~A	
B		X	X		~D
B					D
~B	X			X	D
~B					~D
	~C	C	C	~C	

4

	A	A	~A	~A	
B	X				~D
B	X				D
~B				X	D
~B					~D
	~C	C	C	~C	

PROBLEM: The Veitch Diagram is a method to represent a Boolean expression. A 4x4 grid can represent expressions with at most 4 variables. The method places an X in the cell(s) that describes each term. The ~ symbol is used to show negation. The following rules apply when adding X's to the cells:

1. A term of one variable fills 8 cells. The term ~A fills the 8 cells in Figure #1.
2. A term with 2 variables fills 4 cells. The term A~B fills the 4 cells in Figure #2.
3. A term of 3 variables fills 2 cells. The term BC~D fills the topmost 2 cells in Figure #3.
4. A term of 4 variables fills 1 cell. The term ~A~B~CD fills the single cell in Figure #4.

Variables are eliminated from a term's simplification if the variable and its negation are included. Terms are always joined by the OR symbol (+). AND within terms will always be implied.

Each X can be used just once in the forming of groups. Once the X's are correctly placed in the cells, it's possible to represent expressions. The representation is found by using the following priority rules:

1. Group 8 adjacent X's. This representation is shown in Figure #1. When 8 adjacent X's are grouped the representation is one term. The simplification of Figure #1 is ~A. Priority order is full rows top to bottom, full columns left to right, adjacent end-rows, and finally adjacent end-columns. See Sample #1.
2. Group 4 adjacent X's. This is shown in Figure #2. When 4 adjacent X's are grouped, the representation is 2 terms. Note that C and ~C and D and ~D are eliminated from the representation. The representation of Diagram 2 is A~B. Priority order is full rows, full columns, and finally blocks of 4 in each row left to right, then top to bottom.
3. Group 4 adjacent end-row X's, then 4 adjacent end-column X's. See Sample Input #5. Note that multiple adjacent end rows or end-columns can be combined to form a group of 4 adjacent X's.
4. Group all 4 corners which gives the expression ~C~D.
5. Group 2 adjacent X's. Priority order is top row to bottom row from left to right, then left-most column to right-most column from top to bottom. The term BC~D is the representation for the topmost 2 cells in Figure #3.

Senior Division - Veitch

6. Group 2 adjacent end-row X's for each row from top to bottom, then 2 adjacent end-column X's for each column from left to right. End row adjacent X's are shown in Figure #3. The third row in the diagram has end-row adjacent X's. The representation is ~B~CD.
7. Simplify single X's that always translate to a term of 4 variables. The single X representation for Figure #4 is ~A~B~CD.

INPUT: There will be 5 lines of input (for clarity 10 lines of sample inputs are given). Each line will contain a 4-character string. The 4 characters will each represent a hexadecimal digit. When each is converted to a 4-digit binary number with leading zeros and placed in the diagram from top row to bottom row, the 1's will represent the placement of the X's in the Veitch Diagrams. The input for Figure #3 is 6090 which represents 0110, 0000, 1001 and 0000.

OUTPUT: For each line of input, print the expression according to the rules and priorities above. Since the representation must follow the rules above, the expression must be printed in the exact order shown. Also the factors of each term must be in ABCD order. Spacing between terms and within terms will not affect the answer.

SAMPLE INPUT:
(http://www.datafiles.acsl.org/2020/contest3/sr-sample-input.txt)

```
FF33
00CC
6090
8810
9008
F0B8
9699
8DD8
C3C3
F111
```

SAMPLE OUTPUT:

```
1. B+~A~B
2. A~B
3. BC~D+~B~CD
4. AB~C+~A~B~CD
5. B~C~D+A~B~C~D
6. B~D+~A~BD+A~B~C
7. ~B~C+BCD+B~C~D
8. A~C+ACD+~A~CD
9. AB~D+~ABD+A~BD+~A~B~D
10. B~D+~A~CD+~A~B~C~D
```

Senior Division - Veitch

TEST DATA

TEST INPUT:

F620
F677
910A
4F74
2019

TEST OUTPUT (extra spaces don't matter):

1. B~D + BCD + ~A~BCD
2. C + ~A~B~C + B~C~D
3. ~AB~C + A~C~D + ~A~BC~D
4. BD + ~BCD + AC~D + ~A~B~CD
5. ~A~B~C + ~ABC~D + A~B~C~D

American Computer Science League

2019-2020 Contest #3

INTERMEDIATE DIVISION

1. Boolean Algebra How many ordered triples make the following expression FALSE? $A(\overline{B} + C) + B(A + \overline{C}) + \overline{ABC}$	1.
2. Boolean Algebra Simplify the following expression: $\overline{A(B+C)} + \overline{B}(\overline{A}+C)$	2.
3. Data Structures How many nodes have only one child in the binary search tree for: WINDSORCONNECTICUT	3.
4. Data Structures Given an initially empty stack and the following commands on the stack, what will the next popped item be? PUSH(T), PUSH(H), PUSH(E), PUSH(K), POP(X), POP(X), PUSH(I), PUSH(N), POP(X), PUSH(G), PUSH(A), PUSH(N), POP(X), POP(X), POP(X), PUSH(D), PUSH(I), POP(X), POP(X).	4.

American Computer Science League

2019-2020 Contest #3

INTERMEDIATE DIVISION

5. FSA's and Regular Expressions

5.

Which of the following strings can be produced by the following regular expression?

a b * b a a * b a a

A. a b a b a a
B. a a b b b a a a a b b a a
C. a b a a a b b a a
D. a b b b b a b a
E. a b b b b a a a b a a

American Computer Science League

2019-2020 — **Contest #3**

INTERMEDIATE DIVISION SOLUTIONS

1. Boolean Algebra

$$A(\overline{B} + C) + B(A + \overline{C}) + \overline{ABC}$$

$$= A\overline{B} + AC + AB + B\overline{C} + \overline{A} + \overline{B} + \overline{C}$$

$$= \overline{A} + A\overline{B}(A + 1) + \overline{C}(B + 1) + AC + AB$$

$$= \overline{A} + \overline{B} + \overline{C} + A(B + C)$$

$$\overline{A} + \overline{B} + \overline{C} + A(B + C) = 0$$

$$\rightarrow \overline{A} = 0 \wedge \overline{B} = 0 \wedge \overline{C} = 0 \wedge A(B + C) = 0$$

$$\rightarrow A = 1 \wedge B = 1 \wedge C = 1 \wedge 1 * (1 + 1) = 0$$

which is impossible

So none make it FALSE

1. 0

2. Boolean Algebra

$$\overline{A(B + C)} + \overline{B}(\overline{A} + C)$$

$$= \overline{A} + \overline{B + C} + \overline{A}\overline{B} + \overline{B}C$$

$$= \overline{A} + \overline{B}\overline{C} + \overline{A}\overline{B} + \overline{B}C$$

$$= \overline{A} + \overline{B}(\overline{C} + \overline{A} + C)$$

$$= \overline{A} + \overline{B} \text{ or } \overline{AB}$$

2. $\overline{A} + \overline{B}$ *or* $\overline{AB}$

3. Data Structures

There are 5 with only 1 child: W, C, E, N, C.

The following is the binary search tree for:
WINDSORCONNECTICUT

3. 5

American Computer Science League

2019-2020 — **Contest #3**

INTERMEDIATE DIVISION SOLUTIONS

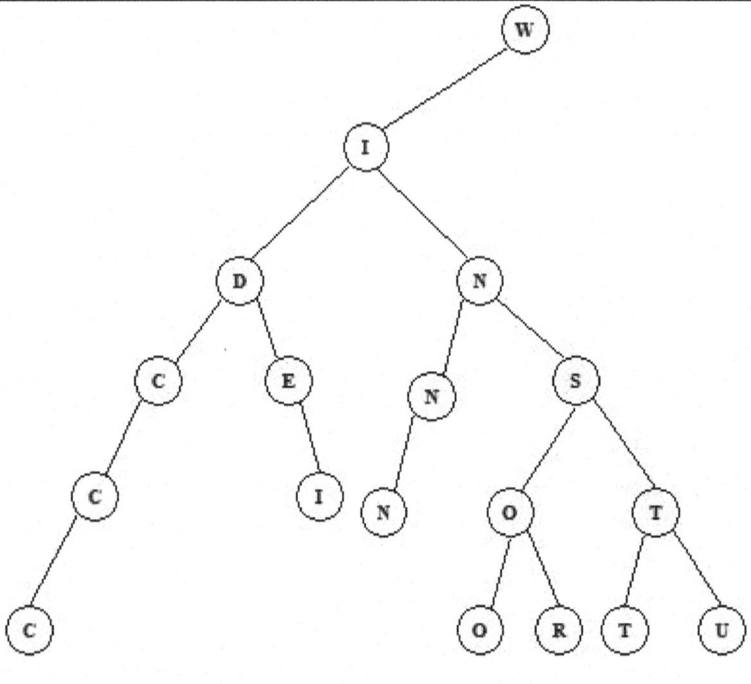

4. Data Structures

The stack is constructed using LIFO as follows:

T, TH, THE, THEK, THE, TH, THI, THIN, THI, THIG, THIGA, THIGAN, THIGA, THIG, THI, THID, THIDI, THID, THI

The next item popped would be I.

4. I

5. FSA's and Regular Expressions

Regular expression: a b * b a a * b a a
The string must start with a single "a" which eliminates B.
It must end with "a b a a" which eliminates C and D.
Both A and E can be formed from the expression.

5. A, E

AMERICAN COMPUTER SCIENCE LEAGUE

2019-2020 **Contest #3**

Intermediate Division - Veitch

1

	A	A	~A	~A	
B			X	X	~D
B			X	X	D
~B			X	X	D
~B			X	X	~D
	~C	C	C	~C	

2

	A	A	~A	~A	
B					~D
B					D
~B	X	X			D
~B	X	X			~D
	~C	C	C	~C	

3

	A	A	~A	~A	
B		X	X		~D
B					D
~B	X			X	D
~B					~D
	~C	C	C	~C	

4

	A	A	~A	~A	
B	X				~D
B	X				D
~B				X	D
~B					~D
	~C	C	C	~C	

PROBLEM: Given a Boolean expression with at most 4 variables, describe its Veitch Diagram. Each Boolean expression will use just the OR operator to combine terms and the terms will be joined using just the AND operator. Note that variables are eliminated from a term's representation if the variable and its negation are included in its grid representation. The Boolean expressions for the Veitch Diagrams in Figures #1 - #4 above are: 1) ~A 2) A~B 3) BC~D + ~BCD 4) AB~C + ~A~B~C D

EXAMPLE: The expression AB + ~C + ~A~D fills the grid in the following way:

5

	A	A	~A	~A	
B	X	X			~D
B	X	X			D
~B					D
~B					~D
	~C	C	C	~C	

6

	A	A	~A	~A	
B	X			X	~D
B	X			X	D
~B	X			X	D
~B	X			X	~D
	~C	C	C	~C	

7

	A	A	~A	~A	
B			X	X	~D
B					D
~B					D
~B			X	X	~D
	~C	C	C	~C	

8

	A	A	~A	~A	
B	X	X	X	X	~D
B	X	X		X	D
~B	X			X	D
~B	X		X	X	~D
	~C	C	C	~C	

AB fills the 4 cells in Figure #5. ~C fills the 8 cells of Figure #6. ~A~D fills the 4 cells of Figure #7. Figure #8 shows all the X's combined in one diagram. Changing the X's in each row to 1's and the blanks to 0's in Figure #8, and then converting the digits to hexadecimal gives FD9B.

INPUT: There will be 5 lines of input (for clarity 10 sample inputs are given). Each line will contain a valid Boolean expression with at most 4 variables. Variables within a term will always be in alphabetical order.

OUTPUT: For each line of input, print a representation of the entries of the Veitch diagram from top to bottom as a string of 4 hexadecimal values.

AMERICAN COMPUTER SCIENCE LEAGUE

2019-2020 **Contest #3**

Intermediate Division - Veitch

SAMPLE INPUT: (http://www.datafiles.acsl.org/2020/contest3/int-sample-input.txt)

```
AB+~AB+~A~B
AB~C~D+AB~CD+~A~B~CD
AB~C~D+~AB~C~D+A~B~C~D
B~D+~B~D
~A~BD+~A~B~D
B~D+~A~BD+A~B~C
~B~C+BCD+B~C~D
A~C+ACD+~A~CD
AB~D+~ABD+A~BD+~A~B~D
B~D+~A~CD+~A~B~C~D
```

SAMPLE OUTPUT:

```
1.  FF33
2.  8810
3.  9008
4.  F00F
5.  0033
6.  F0B8
7.  9699
8.  8DD8
9.  C3C3
10. F111
```

AMERICAN COMPUTER SCIENCE LEAGUE

2019-2020 **Contest #3**

Intermediate Division - Veitch

TEST DATA

TEST INPUT:

~A~B+AB+~CD+C~D
B~D+AC+~A~B+CD
~ABD+~BCD+D
~A~BD+~A~BD+AC+BD
~ABC~D+A~B~C~D+~A~B~C

TEST OUTPUT:

1. EDB7
2. F677
3. 0FF0
4. 4F74
5. 2019

American Computer Science League

2019-2020 — **Contest #3**

JUNIOR DIVISION

1. Boolean Algebra

Simplify the following expression:

$$A(\overline{AB}) + \overline{A}\left(\overline{A+B}\right) + A + \overline{B}$$

1.

2. Boolean Algebra

Which ordered triples make the following FALSE?

$$\overline{A\ B}\ C + A\ \overline{B}\ C + \overline{A\ B\ \overline{C}}$$

2.

3. Data Structures

What is the depth of the binary search tree for:

THECONSTITUTIONSTATE

3.

4. Data Structures

Given an initially empty queue and the following commands on the queue, what will the next popped item be?

PUSH(L), PUSH(E), PUSH(S), POP(X), PUSH(M), PUSH(I), PUSH(S), POP(X), POP(X), PUSH(E), PUSH(R), PUSH(A), POP(X), POP(X), PUSH(B), PUSH(L), POP(X), POP(X), PUSH(E), POP(X), POP(X), PUSH(S).

4.

American Computer Science League

2019-2020 Contest #3

JUNIOR DIVISION

5. What Does This Program Do? - Arrays

What is outputted when this program is run?

```
for i = 1 to 5
    for j = 1 to 5
        a(i,j) = int((i + j) / 2)
    next j
next i
for i = 1 to 5
    for j = 1 to 5
        if a(i,j) / 2 == int(a(i,j) / 2) then
            a(i,j) = a(i,j) / 2
        else
            a(i,j) = 2 * a(i,j)
        end if
    next j
next i
for i = 1 to 5
    for j = 1 to 4
        if a(i,j)  ==  a(i, j + 1) then
            a(i,j) = 0
        end if
    next j
next i
print a(1,5) + a(5,5)
end
```

5.

American Computer Science League

2019-2020 **Contest #3**

JUNIOR DIVISION SOLUTIONS

---

1. Boolean Algebra

$$A(\overline{AB}) + \overline{A}\left(\overline{A+B}\right) + A + \overline{B}$$
$$= A(\overline{A} + \overline{B}) + \overline{A}\,\overline{A}\,\overline{B} + A + \overline{B}$$
$$= A\overline{A} + A\overline{B} + \overline{A}\,\overline{B} + A + \overline{B}$$
$$= 0 + A(\overline{B} + 1) + \overline{B}(\overline{A} + 1)$$
$$= A + \overline{B}$$

1. $A + \overline{B}$

---

2. Boolean Algebra

$$\overline{A\,B}\,C + A\,\overline{B}\,C + \overline{A\,B\,\overline{C}}$$
$$= \left(\overline{A} + \overline{B}\right)C + A\,\overline{B}\,C + \overline{A} + \overline{B} + C$$
$$= \overline{A}\,C + \overline{B}\,C + A\,\overline{B}\,C + \overline{A} + \overline{B} + C$$
$$= \overline{B}(C + A\,C + 1) + \overline{A}(C + 1) + C$$
$$= \overline{B} + \overline{A} + C$$
$$\overline{A} + \overline{B} + C = 0 \rightarrow \overline{A} = 0 \wedge \overline{B} = 0 \wedge C = 0$$
$$\rightarrow A = 1,\ B = 1,\ C = 0 \rightarrow (1,\ 1,\ 0)$$

2. (1, 1, 0)

American Computer Science League

2019-2020 Contest #3

JUNIOR DIVISION SOLUTIONS

3. Data Structures

The depth of the tree for THECONSTITUTIONSTATE is 8.

The binary search tree is:

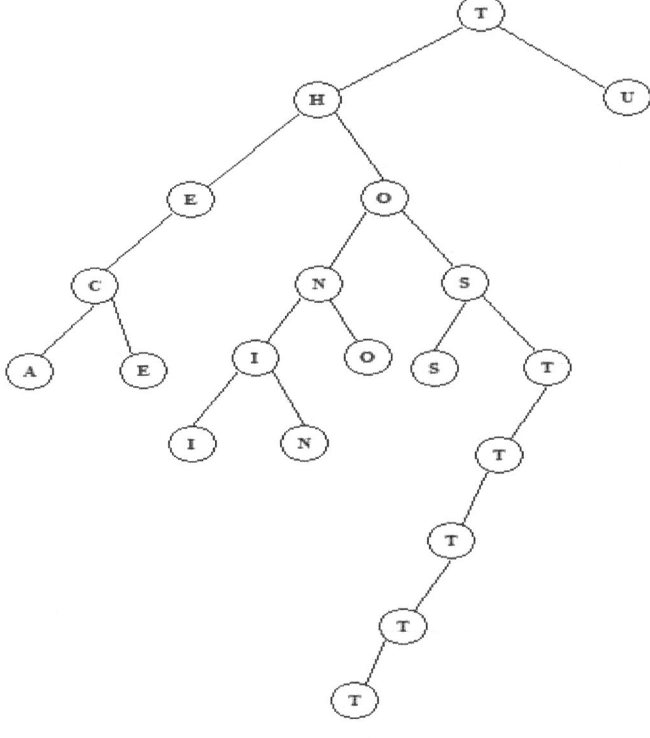

3. 8

4. Data Structures

The queue is constructed using FIFO as follows:

L, LE, LES, ES, ESM, ESMI, ESMIS, SMIS, MIS, MISE,

MISER, MISERA, ISERA, SERA, SERAB, SERABL,

ERABL, RABL, RABLE, ABLE, BLE, BLES

The next item popped would be B.

4. B

American Computer Science League

2019-2020 Contest #3

JUNIOR DIVISION SOLUTIONS

5. What Does This Program Do? - Arrays

Array formed by first nested loop:

1	1	2	2	3
1	2	2	3	3
2	2	3	3	4
2	3	3	4	4
3	3	4	4	5

Array from 2nd nested loop:

2	2	1	1	6
2	1	1	6	6
1	1	6	6	2
1	6	6	2	2
6	6	2	2	10

Array from 3rd nested loop:

0	2	0	1
2	0	1	0
0	1	0	6
1	0	6	0
0	6	0	2

a(1,5) + a(5,5) = 6 + 10 = 16

5. 16

AMERICAN COMPUTER SCIENCE LEAGUE

2019-2020 **Contest #3**

Junior Division - Veitch

1

	A	A	~A	~A
B			X	X
~B			X	X
	~C	C	C	~C

2

	A	A	~A	~A
B				
~B	X	X	X	X
	~C	C	C	~C

3

	A	A	~A	~A
B			X	X
~B	X	X		
	~C	C	C	~C

4

	A	A	~A	~A
B	X			X
~B		X		
	~C	C	C	~C

PROBLEM: The Veitch Diagram is a method to represent a Boolean expression. The method places an X in the cell that describes each term and groups adjacent cells. For this program, the X's are already placed. Each diagram will represent an expression of at most 3 variables. Variables are eliminated from a term's representation if the variable and its negation are included. Terms are always joined by the OR symbol (+). AND within terms will always be implied. Each X can be used just once in the forming of groups. The ~ symbol will be used to indicate NOT.

X's are grouped according to the following priorities:

1. Group 4 adjacent X's. This is shown in Diagrams 1 and 2. When 4 adjacent X's are grouped, the representation is one term. The representation of Diagram 1 is ~A. Note B and ~B and then C and ~C are included in the grouped X's and are eliminated. The priority for grouping 4 adjacent X's is top row, then bottom row, and finally columns from left to right. The representation of Diagram 2 is ~B.

2. Group 4 end column adjacent X's. That is X's fill the first and last column. There is only one way that this can be done which yields ~C.

3. Group 2 adjacent X's. When 2 adjacent X's are grouped, the result is a term of 2 variables. In Diagram 3 there are 2 groups of 2 adjacent X's. The priority for grouping 2 adjacent X's is top row from left to right, bottom row from left to right, and then columns from left to right. The top row representation is ~AB. The bottom row representation is A~B. The expression for Diagram 3 is ~AB + A~B.

4. Group 2 end column adjacent X's. The priority is top row adjacent X's first. This is shown in Diagram 4. The top row in the diagram has end column adjacent X's. That part of the representation is B~C.

5. Represent single X's in the priority top row, bottom row, and then left to right. Diagram 4 has a single X that is not already used by the above rules. Single X's always translate to a term of 3 variables. It translates to A~BC. The expression for Diagram 4 is B~C + A~BC.

AMERICAN COMPUTER SCIENCE LEAGUE

2019-2020 **Contest #3**

Junior Division - Veitch

INPUT: There will be 5 lines of input. Each line will contain a 2-character string. The 2 characters will each represent a hexadecimal digit. When each is converted to a 4-digit binary number with leading zeros and placed into the diagram top row then bottom row, the 1's will represent the placement of the X's in the Veitch Diagram. The input for Diagram 4 is 94 which represents 1001 and 0100.

OUTPUT: For each line of input, print the expression using the rules and priorities above. Since the listed priorities apply, the terms must be listed in the order specified. Also, the factors must always be in ABC order. Spacing between terms and within terms will not affect the answer.

SAMPLE INPUT: **SAMPLE OUTPUT:**
(http://www.datafiles.acsl.org/2020/contest3/jr-sample-input.txt)

33	1. ~A
3C	2. ~AB + A~B
94	3. B~C + A~BC
77	4. C + ~A~C
95	5. ~A~C + AB~C + A~BC

AMERICAN COMPUTER SCIENCE LEAGUE

2019-2020 **Contest #3**

Junior Division - Veitch

TEST DATA

TEST INPUT:

F0
1D
9D
E9
E7

TEST OUTPUT (spaces are optional):

1. B
2. A~B + ~A~C
3. ~C + A~BC
4. AB + ~B~C + ~ABC
5. C + AB~C + ~A~B~C

American Computer Science League

2019-2020 — **Contest #3**

ELEMENTARY DIVISION

1. Boolean Algebra Determine whether this Boolean expression is TRUE or FALSE: NOT (7 > 4 + 3) AND (5 * 3 ≥ 7 * 2 OR 12 - 7 ≠ 9 - 4)	**1.**
2. Boolean Algebra What ordered pair(s) make the following expression TRUE? (A OR NOT B) AND NOT (A AND B)	**2.**
3. Boolean Algebra How many ordered pairs make both of these expressions FALSE? ~(A AND ~B) ~(~A OR B)	**3.**
4. Boolean Algebra Simplify the following Boolean expression to the fewest operators: ~A(A~B + ~A~B) + ~B(A~B + ~A~B)	**4.**
5. Boolean Algebra Which of the following are equivalent Boolean expressions: A. ~(A + ~B) + AB B. B~A + ~(A + B) C. ~A~B + ~BA D. ~B(A + ~(AB))	**5.**

American Computer Science League

2019-2020 — Contest #3

ELEMENTARY DIVISION SOLUTIONS

1. Boolean Algebra NOT (7 > 4 + 3) AND (5 * 3 ≥ 7 * 2 OR 12 - 7 ≠ 9 - 4) = NOT FALSE AND (15 ≥ 14 OR 5 ≠ 5) = TRUE AND (TRUE OR FALSE) = TRUE AND TRUE = **TRUE**	**1.** TRUE
2. Boolean Algebra (see table below)	**2.** (0,0) and (1,0) in either order
3. Boolean Algebra ~(A AND ~B) is FALSE when A AND ~B is TRUE which means A = 1 and B = 0. ~(~A OR B) is FALSE when ~A OR B is TRUE which means A = 0 or B = 1. (1,0) in the 1st expression can't possibly work for the 2nd expression.	**3.** 0
4. Boolean Algebra ~A(A~B + ~A~B) + ~B(A~B + ~A~B) = ~AA~B + ~A~A~B + ~BA~B + ~B~A~B = 0 + ~A~B + A~B + ~A~B = ~A~B + A~B = ~B(~A + A) = ~B(1) = **~B**	**4.** ~B

Table for problem 2:

A	B	~B	A+~B	AB	~(AB)	(A+~B)(~(AB))
0	**0**	1	1	0	1	1
0	1	0	0	0	1	0
1	**0**	1	1	0	1	1
1	1	0	1	1	0	0

American Computer Science League

2019-2020 Contest #3

ELEMENTARY DIVISION SOLUTIONS

5. Boolean Algebra A. ~(A + ~B) + AB = ~AB + AB = B B. B~A + ~(A + B) = ~AB + ~A~B = ~A C. ~A~B + ~BA = ~A~B + A~B = **~B** D. ~B(A + ~A) = A~B + ~A~B = **~B**	**5.** C and D

American Computer Science League

2019-2020 ——— **Contest #3**

CLASSROOM DIVISION

1. Boolean Algebra Simplify the following expression: $A(\overline{AB}) + \overline{A}(\overline{A+B}) + A + \overline{B}$	**1.**
2. Boolean Algebra Which ordered triples make the following FALSE? $\overline{A\ B}\ C + A\ \overline{B}\ C + \overline{A\ B\ \overline{C}}$	**2.**
3. Data Structures What is the depth of the binary search tree for: **THECONSTITUTIONSTATE**	**3.**
4. Data Structures Given an initially empty queue and the following commands on the queue, what will the next popped item be? PUSH(L), PUSH(E), PUSH(S), POP(X), PUSH(M), PUSH(I), PUSH(S), POP(X), POP(X), PUSH(E), PUSH(R), PUSH(A), POP(X), POP(X), PUSH(B), PUSH(L), POP(X), POP(X), PUSH(E), POP(X), POP(X), PUSH(S).	**4.**

American Computer Science League

2019-2020 — Contest #3

CLASSROOM DIVISION

---

5. What Does This Program Do? - Arrays

5.

What is outputted when this program is run?

```
for i = 1 to 5
    for j = 1 to 5
        a(i,j) = int((i + j) / 2)
    next j
next i
for i = 1 to 5
    for j = 1 to 5
        if a(i,j) / 2 == int(a(i,j) / 2) then
            a(i,j) = a(i,j) / 2
        else
            a(i,j) = 2 * a(i,j)
        end if
    next j
next i
for i = 1 to 5
    for j = 1 to 4
        if a(i,j)  ==  a(i, j + 1) then
            a(i,j) = 0
        end if
    next j
next i
print a(1,5) + a(5,5)
end
```

American Computer Science League

2019-2020 **Contest #3**

CLASSROOM DIVISION

6. Boolean Algebra How many ordered triples make the following expression FALSE? $A(\overline{B} + C) + B(A + \overline{C}) + \overline{ABC}$	**6.**
7. Boolean Algebra Simplify the following expression: $\overline{A(B+C)} + \overline{B}(\overline{A}+C)$	**7.**
8. Data Structures How many nodes have only one child in the binary search tree for: WINDSORCONNECTICUT	**8.**
9. Data Structures Given an initially empty stack and the following commands on the stack, what will the next popped item be? PUSH(T), PUSH(H), PUSH(E), PUSH(K), POP(X), POP(X), PUSH(I), PUSH(N), POP(X), PUSH(G), PUSH(A), PUSH(N), POP(X), POP(X), POP(X), PUSH(D), PUSH(I), POP(X), POP(X).	**9.**

American Computer Science League

2019-2020 — Contest #3

CLASSROOM DIVISION

---

10. FSA's and Regular Expressions | **10.**

Which of the following strings can be produced by the following regular expression?

a b * b a a * b a a

A. a b a b a a
B. a a b b b a a a a b b a a
C. a b a a a b b a a
D. a b b b b a b a
E. a b b b b a a a b a a

American Computer Science League

2019-2020 **Contest #3**

CLASSROOM DIVISION SOLUTIONS

1. Boolean Algebra $A(\overline{AB}) + \overline{A}(\overline{A+B}) + A + \overline{B}$ $= A(\overline{A} + \overline{B}) + \overline{A}\,\overline{A}\,\overline{B} + A + \overline{B}$ $= A\overline{A} + A\overline{B} + \overline{A}\,\overline{B} + A + \overline{B}$ $= 0 + A(\overline{B} + 1) + \overline{B}(\overline{A} + 1)$ $= A + \overline{B}$	**1.** $A + \overline{B}$
2. Boolean Algebra $\overline{A\,B}\,C + A\,\overline{B}\,C + \overline{A\,B\,\overline{C}}$ $= (\overline{A} + \overline{B})C + A\,\overline{B}\,C + \overline{A} + \overline{B} + C$ $= \overline{A}\,C + \overline{B\,C} + A\,\overline{B}\,C + \overline{A} + \overline{B} + C$ $= \overline{B}(C + A\,C + 1) + \overline{A}(C + 1) + C$ $= \overline{B} + \overline{A} + C$ $\overline{A} + \overline{B} + C = 0 \rightarrow \overline{A} = 0 \wedge \overline{B} = 0 \wedge C = 0$ $\rightarrow A = 1,\ B = 1,\ C = 0 \rightarrow (1,\ 1,\ 0)$	**2.** (1, 1, 0)

American Computer Science League

2019-2020 **Contest #3**

CLASSROOM DIVISION SOLUTIONS

3. Data Structures The depth of the tree for THECONSTITUTIONSTATE is 8. The binary search tree is:	**3.** 8

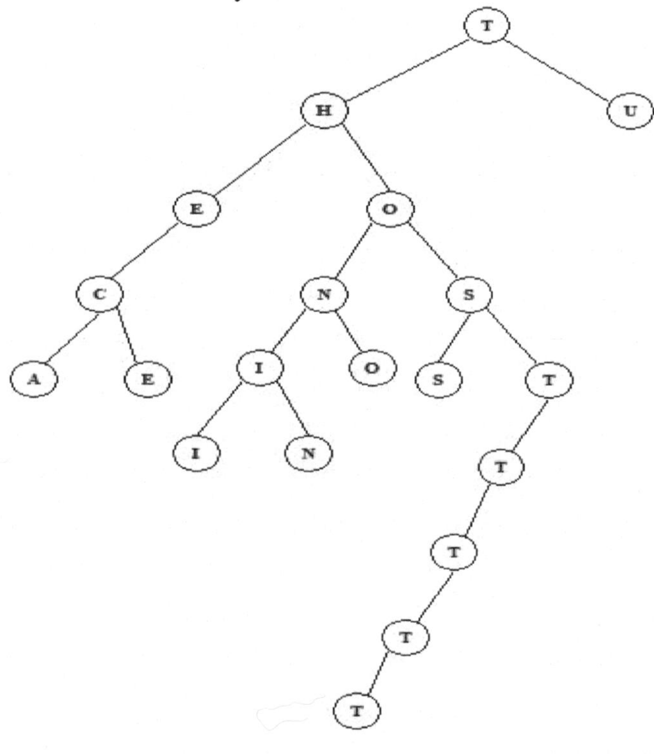

4. Data Structures The queue is constructed using FIFO as follows: L, LE, LES, ES, ESM, ESMI, ESMIS, SMIS, MIS, MISE, MISER, MISERA, ISERA, SERA, SERAB, SERABL, ERABL, RABL, RABLE, ABLE, BLE, BLES The next item popped would be B.	**4.** B

American Computer Science League

2019-2020 Contest #3

CLASSROOM DIVISION SOLUTIONS

5. What Does This Program Do? - Arrays

Array formed by first nested loop:

1	1	2	2	3
1	2	2	3	3
2	2	3	3	4
2	3	3	4	4
3	3	4	4	5

Array from 2nd nested loop:

2	2	1	1	6
2	1	1	6	6
1	1	6	6	2
1	6	6	2	2
6	6	2	2	10

Array from 3rd nested loop:

0	2	0	1
2	0	1	0
0	1	0	6
1	0	6	0
0	6	0	2

a(1,5) + a(5,5) = 6 + 10 = 16

5. 16

American Computer Science League

2019-2020 — **Contest #3**

CLASSROOM DIVISION SOLUTIONS

6. Boolean Algebra

$$A(\overline{B} + C) + B(A + \overline{C}) + \overline{ABC}$$
$$= A\overline{B} + AC + AB + B\overline{C} + \overline{A} + \overline{B} + \overline{C}$$
$$= \overline{A} + A\overline{B}(A + 1) + \overline{C}(B + 1) + AC + AB$$
$$= \overline{A} + \overline{B} + \overline{C} + A(B + C)$$
$$\overline{A} + \overline{B} + \overline{C} + A(B + C) = 0$$
$$\rightarrow \overline{A} = 0 \wedge \overline{B} = 0 \wedge \overline{C} = 0 \wedge A(B + C) = 0$$
$$\rightarrow A = 1 \wedge B = 1 \wedge C = 1 \wedge 1 * (1 + 1) = 0$$

which is impossible

So none make it FALSE

6. 0

7. Boolean Algebra

$$\overline{A(B + C)} + \overline{B}(\overline{A} + C)$$
$$= \overline{A} + \overline{B + C} + \overline{A}\overline{B} + \overline{B}C$$
$$= \overline{A} + \overline{B}\overline{C} + \overline{A}\overline{B} + \overline{B}C$$
$$= \overline{A} + \overline{B}(\overline{C} + \overline{A} + C)$$
$$= \overline{A} + \overline{B} \text{ or } \overline{AB}$$

7. $\overline{A} + \overline{B}$ *or* $\overline{AB}$

8. Data Structures

There are 5 with only 1 child: W, C, E, N, C.

The following is the binary search tree for:
WINDSORCONNECTICUT

8. 5

American Computer Science League

2019-2020 — **Contest #3**

CLASSROOM DIVISION SOLUTIONS

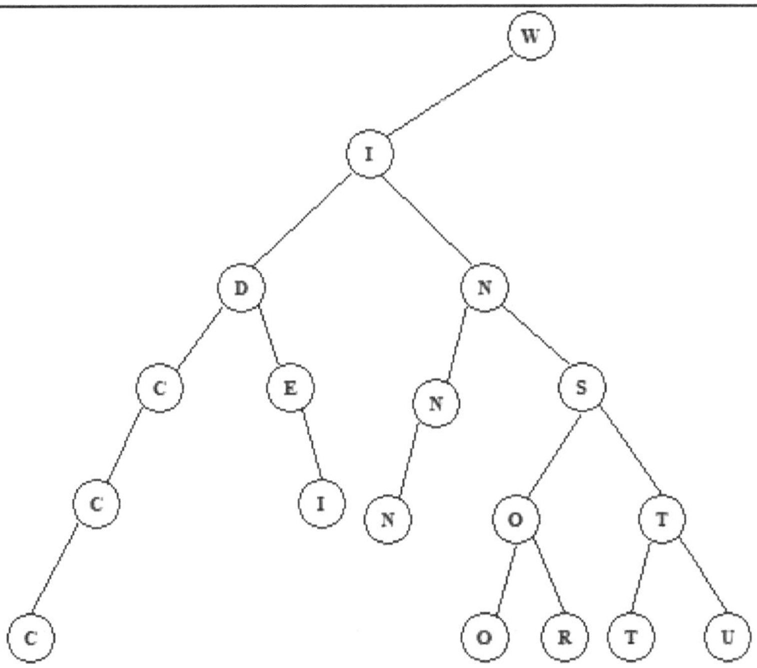

9. Data Structures The stack is constructed using LIFO as follows: T, TH, THE, THEK, THE, TH, THI, THIN, THI, THIG, THIGA, THIGAN, THIGA, THIG, THI, THID, THIDI, THID, THI The next item popped would be I.	**9.** I
10. FSA's and Regular Expressions Regular expression: a b * b a a * b a a The string must start with a single "a" which eliminates B. It must end with "a b a a" which eliminates C and D. Both A and E can be formed from the expression.	**10.** A, E

Contest #4

American Computer Science League

2019-2020 Contest #4

SENIOR DIVISION

1. Graph Theory How many paths of length 3 from Vertex C in the following directed graph? 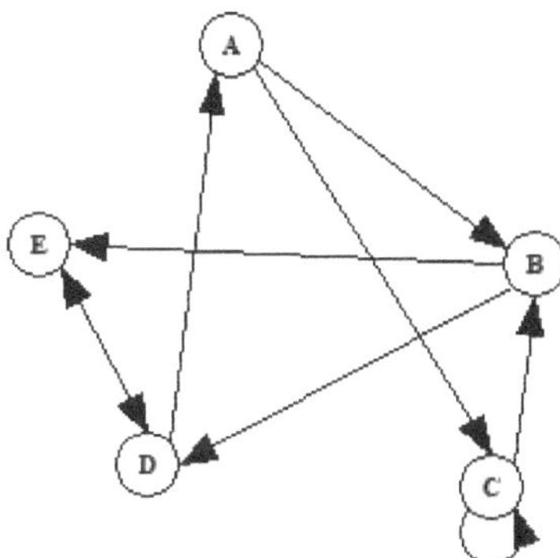 	1.
2. Graph Theory How many cycles are there from Vertex B in the following directed graph? 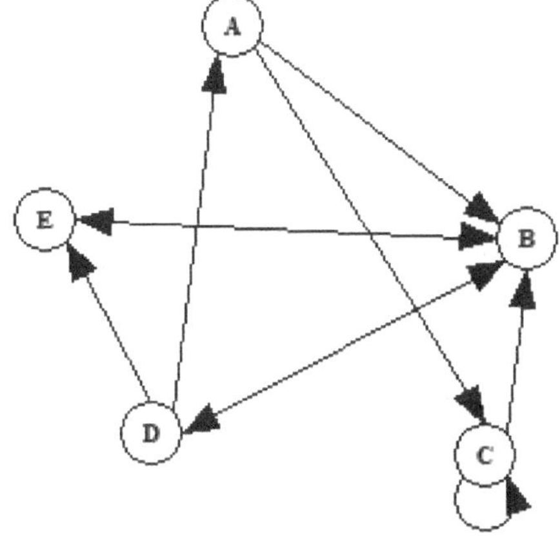 	2.

American Computer Science League

2019-2020 Contest #4

SENIOR DIVISION

3. Digital Electronics	3.
4. Digital Electronics	4.

3. Digital Electronics

Simply the Boolean expression represented by the following digital circuit:

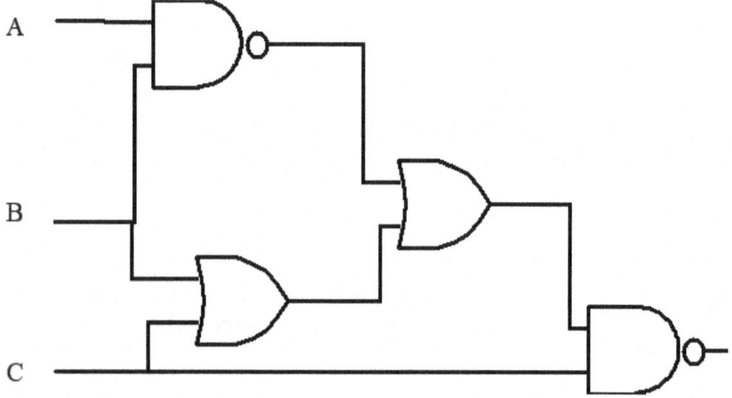

4. Digital Electronics

How many ordered quadruples make the following digital circuit FALSE?

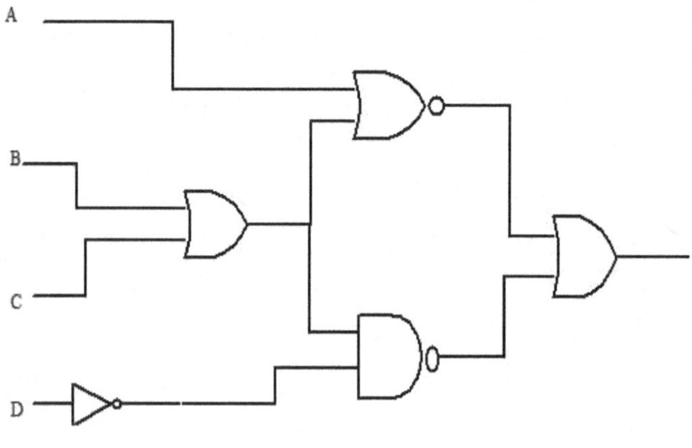

American Computer Science League

2019-2020 Contest #4

SENIOR DIVISION

5. Assembly Language 5.

What would be output when this program is executed?

```
      X    DC     1
      Z    DC     0
TOP   LOAD        X
      MULT        X
      ADD         Z
      STORE       Z
      SUB         = 500
      BL          P
      LOAD        X
      PRINT       X
      END
  P   LOAD        X
      ADD         = 1
      STORE       X
      BU          TOP
```

American Computer Science League

2019-2020 **Contest #4**

SENIOR DIVISION SOLUTIONS

1. Graph Theory

0	1	1	0	0
0	0	0	1	1
0	1	1	0	0
1	0	0	0	1
0	0	0	1	0

3 =

1	1	1	2	2
1	1	1	1	1
1	1	1	2	2
1	1	1	1	2
0	1	1	1	0

There are 7 from C: 1 from C to A, 1 from C to B, 1 from C to C, 2 from C to D and 2 from C to E. The answer is found by adding the values in the 3rd row.

1. 7

2. Graph Theory

There are 5 cycles: BDB, BEB, BDAB, BDEB, BDACB.

2. 5

3. Digital Electronics

The digital circuit translates to:

$$\overline{(AB + (B + C))\,C}$$
$$= \overline{AB + (B + C)} + \overline{C}$$
$$= \overline{AB}\,\overline{(B + C)} + \overline{C}$$
$$= (\overline{A} + \overline{B})\,\overline{B}\,\overline{C} + \overline{C}$$
$$= \overline{A}\,\overline{B}\,\overline{C} + \overline{B}\,\overline{C} + \overline{C}$$
$$= \overline{C}\,(\overline{A}\,\overline{B} + \overline{B} + 1)$$
$$= \overline{C}$$

3. $\overline{C}$
or NOT C
or ~C

4. Digital Electronics

The digital circuit translates to:

$$\overline{(A + (B + C))} + \overline{(B + C)\overline{D}}$$
$$= \overline{A}\,\overline{(B + C)} + \overline{(B + C)} + \overline{\overline{D}}$$
$$= \overline{A}\,\overline{B}\,\overline{C} + \overline{B}\,\overline{C} + D$$
$$= \overline{B}\,\overline{C}\,(\overline{A} + 1) + D$$
$$= \overline{B}\,\overline{C} + D$$

To be FALSE, all terms are FALSE.

$A = *,\ D = 0,\ \overline{B}\,\overline{C} = 0$

$\Rightarrow (B=1 \wedge C=1) \vee (B=1 \wedge C=0) \vee (B=0 \wedge C=1)$

Therefore, 6 quadruples make it FALSE:
(0, 0, 1, 0), (1, 0, 1, 0), (0, 1, 0, 0), (1, 1, 0, 0), (0, 1, 1, 0), (1, 1, 1, 0)

4. 6

5. Assembly Language

The assembly programs can be converted to an equivalent program as follows:

```
X = 1
Z = 0
Z = Z + X * X
WHILE Z < 500
      X = X + 1
      Z = Z + X * X
END WHILE
PRINT X
END
```

This programs add the squares of the natural numbers until sum is greater than 500. This occurs when X = 11.

5. 11

2019-2020 **AMERICAN COMPUTER SCIENCE LEAGUE** Contest #4

Senior Division - Patolli

PROBLEM: Given the grid below for the game of ACSL Patolli, utilize the following rules to play the game. All rules must be applied in the sequential order listed.

1. There are 2 players. Each player has 3 markers.
2. The markers move according to the roll of a die (1 – 6).
3. Markers move in numerical order around the grid.
4. If, on a die roll, a marker lands on an occupied location, then that marker loses its turn and remains at its previous location.
5. A marker can jump over another marker on its way to finish its move.
6. A marker finishes its way around the grid when it lands on location 52. It is then removed from the board. A move can't take a marker beyond location 52. If it does, the marker remains at its previous location.
7. If, on a die roll, a marker lands on an unoccupied location that is a prime number, the marker then moves six locations forward. However, it stops immediately before any occupied location.
8. If, on a die roll, a marker lands on an unoccupied location that is a perfect square greater than 4, the marker then moves 6 locations backwards. However, it stops immediately before any occupied location.
9. If, on a die roll, a marker lands on an unoccupied location that is neither a prime number nor a perfect square, then determine if the marker made at least one horizontal move followed by at least one vertical move (such as going from 6 to 8, 11 to 13, 26 to 28 … but not 2 to 4 or 30 to 32). In that case, the marker can only land on a location on its path that is a multiple of the die roll value even if it moves a smaller distance than the die roll value. However, if all the locations in its path that are multiples are occupied, then the marker does not move from its current location. The rules listed in #7 and #8 do not apply when using #9.

				1	52				
				2	51				
7	6	5	4	3	50	49	48	47	46
8	9	10	11	12	41	42	43	44	45
17	16	15	14	13	40	39	38	37	36
18	19	20	21	22	31	32	33	34	35
				23	30				
				24	29				
				25	28				
				26	27				

2019-2020 **AMERICAN COMPUTER SCIENCE LEAGUE** Contest #4

Senior Division - Patolli

For this program, markers will be moved alternately by the opponent and then by the player. All of the marker moves will be by the marker at the opponent's lowest numbered location and then by the player's marker at the lowest numbered location.

Using Sample #1, the opponent's markers are at Locations #3, 15 and 18. The player's markers are at Locations #5, 13 and 21. The opponent's lowest numbered marker moves first. It is at Location #3. The die roll is 4. It moves to Location #7. 7 is a prime. It tries to move 6 locations forward, but it is blocked so it stops at Location #12. The player's lowest numbered marker is at Location #5. The die roll is 5. It moves to Location #10. The move went from at least 1 horizontal move (6 to 7) to at least 1 vertical move (7 to 8), so the marker must land on a multiple of 5. It did. The next die roll is 4. The opponent's marker at Location #12 moves to Location #16. 16 is a perfect square. The marker tries to move backwards 6 locations, but it is blocked at Location #15, so it does not move. The next die roll is 4. The player's marker is at Location #10, but the move went from at least 1 horizontal move (11 to 12) to at least 1 vertical move (12 to 13), so the marker must land on a multiple of 4. It stops at Location #12. The opponent's markers are at Locations #15, 16 and 18. The player's markers are at Locations #12, 13 and 21.

INPUT: There will be 5 lines of input. Each line will contain the 3 values giving the locations of the opponent's markers on the board. That will be followed by the location of the 3 player's markers. That will be followed by an integer r, giving the number of die rolls. That will be followed by the value of those die rolls.

OUTPUT: For each line of input, print the sum of the opponent's marker locations and the sum of the player's marker locations. If a marker was removed from the board, it is not part of the sum.

SAMPLE INPUT:	**SAMPLE OUTPUT:**
http://www.datafiles.acsl.org/2020/contest4/sr-sample-input.txt	
3 15 18 5 13 21 4 4 5 4 4	1. 49 46
1 11 20 3 7 16 8 3 5 6 4 6 6 6 1	2. 51 34
18 22 15 6 10 5 6 3 2 6 5 1 4	3. 55 37
12 20 15 40 35 30 5 1 2 3 4 5	4. 54 111
25 20 15 12 9 6 7 6 5 4 5 3 1 6	5. 71 33

2019-2020 **AMERICAN COMPUTER SCIENCE LEAGUE** Contest #4

Senior Division - Patolli

TEST DATA

TEST INPUT:

1 9 18 3 10 17 8 3 1 6 4 6 6 5 5
40 44 48 50 30 45 12 5 3 1 2 4 6 5 4 3 2 1 6
38 41 48 34 42 46 10 6 6 5 1 6 3 5 1 5 2
4 20 38 12 23 44 10 5 6 4 6 3 6 3 4 4 3
17 34 41 15 29 39 16 6 1 5 1 4 6 2 3 5 1 5 5 5 3 3 6

TEST OUTPUT:

1. 31 44
2. 144 138
3. 145 135
4. 85 113
5. 138 124

American Computer Science League

2019-2020 Contest #4

INTERMEDIATE DIVISION

1. Graph Theory After drawing the following directed graph, how many pairs of different vertices have no edge in either direction between them? Vertices: {A, B ,C, D, E, F} and Edges: {AB, FD, CC, EA, FE, AC, DB, FA, CB, EE, BD}	1.
2. Graph Theory How many more paths of length 3 are there than of length 2 in this directed graph? 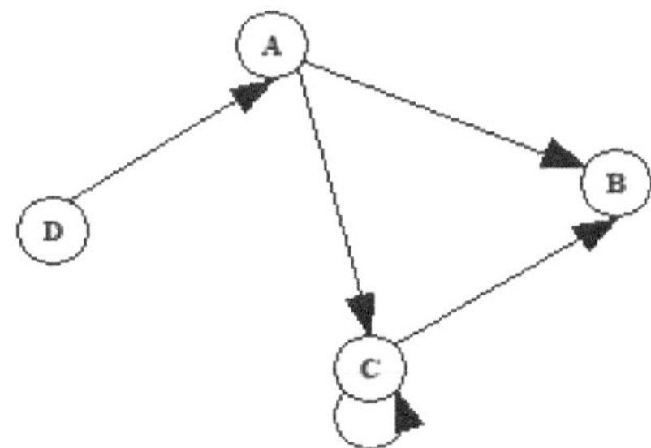 	2.
3. Digital Electronics Simplify the Boolean expression represented by the following digital circuit. Perform all indicated operations. 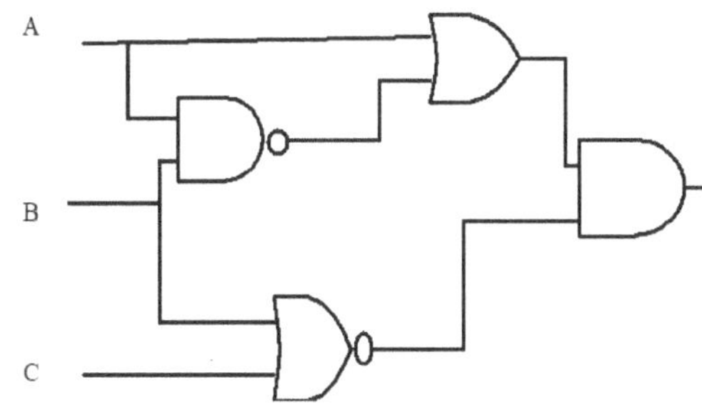 	3.

4. Digital Electronics

4.

How many ordered triples make the Boolean expression represented by this digital circuit TRUE?

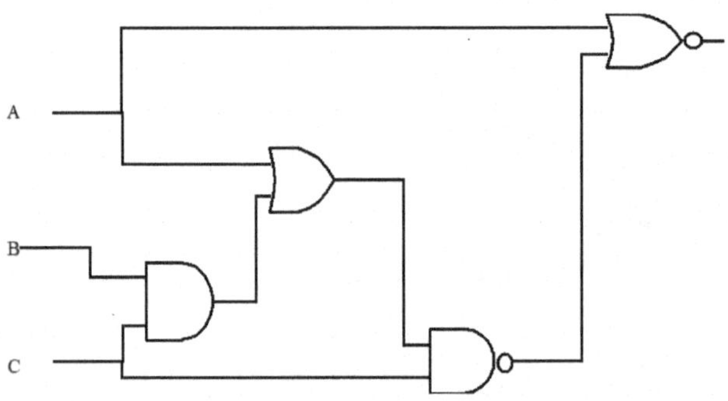

5. Assembly Language

5.

What is output when this program is executed?

```
      X  DC    8
      Y  DC    15
TOP   LOAD     X
      MULT     X
      SUB      Y
      BL       L
      LOAD     X
      SUB      =1
      STORE    X
      LOAD     Y
      SUB      =1
      STORE    Y
      BU       TOP
  L   PRINT    X
      END
```

American Computer Science League

2019-2020 Contest #4

INTERMEDIATE DIVISION SOLUTIONS

1. Graph Theory

There are 7 different pairs of vertices with no direct edge between them:

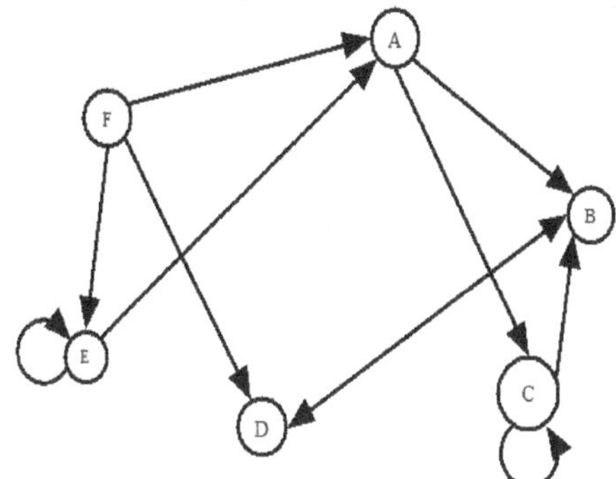

AD, BE, BF, CD, CE, CF, and DE.

1. 7

2. Graph Theory

$$M = \begin{bmatrix} 0 & 1 & 1 & 0 \\ 0 & 0 & 0 & 0 \\ 0 & 1 & 1 & 0 \\ 1 & 0 & 0 & 0 \end{bmatrix} \quad M^2 = \begin{bmatrix} 0 & 1 & 1 & 0 \\ 0 & 0 & 0 & 0 \\ 0 & 1 & 1 & 0 \\ 0 & 1 & 1 & 0 \end{bmatrix} \quad M^3 = \begin{bmatrix} 0 & 1 & 1 & 0 \\ 0 & 0 & 0 & 0 \\ 0 & 1 & 1 & 0 \\ 0 & 1 & 1 & 0 \end{bmatrix}$$

There are 6 paths of length 2 and 6 paths of length 3. The difference is 0.

2. 0

3. Digital Electronics

The digital circuit translates to:

$$(A + \overline{AB})\left(\overline{B + C}\right)$$
$$= (A + \overline{A} + \overline{B})\ \overline{B}\,\overline{C}$$
$$= \left(1 + \overline{B}\right)\overline{B}\,\overline{C}$$
$$= \overline{B}\,\overline{C}$$

3. $\overline{B}\,\overline{C}$ or $\overline{B + C}$

Either answer is accepted.

4. Digital Electronics

The digital circuit translates to:

$$\overline{A + \overline{(A + BC)\,C}}$$

$$= \overline{A}(A + BC)\,C$$

$$= \overline{A}AC + \overline{A}BC$$

$$= 0 + \overline{A}BC$$

$$= \overline{A}BC$$

So (0,1,1) makes it TRUE.

4. 1

5. Assembly Language

An equivalent program using our WDTPD language is:

```
X = 8
Y = 15
while X * X - Y >= 0
   X = X - 1
   Y = Y - 1
end while
output X
```

X	8	7	6	5	4	3
Y	15	14	13	12	11	10
X*X-Y	49	35	23	13	5	-1

5. 3

Intermediate Division - Patolli

PROBLEM: Given the grid below for the game of ACSL Patolli, utilize the following rules to play the game. All rules must be applied in the sequential order listed.

1. There are 2 players. Each player has 3 markers.
2. The markers move according to the roll of a die (1 – 6).
3. Markers move in numerical order around the grid.
4. If, on a die roll, a marker lands on an occupied location, then that marker loses its turn and remains at its previous location.
5. A marker can jump over another marker on its way to finish its move.
6. A marker finishes its way around the grid when it lands on location 52. It is then removed from the board. A move can't take a marker beyond location 52. If it does, the marker remains at its previous location.
7. If, on a die roll, a marker lands on an unoccupied location that is a prime number, the marker then moves six locations forward. However, it stops immediately before any occupied location.
8. If, on a die roll, a marker lands on an unoccupied location that is a perfect square greater than 4, the marker then moves 6 locations backwards. However, it stops immediately before any occupied location.
9. If, on a die roll, a marker lands on an unoccupied location that is neither a prime number nor a perfect square, then determine if the marker made at least one horizontal move followed by at least one vertical move (such as going from 6 to 8, 11 to 13, 26 to 28 … but not 2 to 4 or 30 to 32). In that case, the marker can only land on a location on its path that is a multiple of the die roll value even if it moves a smaller distance than the die roll value. However, if all the locations in its path that are multiples are occupied, then the marker does not move from its current location. The rules listed in #7 and #8 do not apply when using #9.

				1	52				
				2	51				
7	6	5	4	3	50	49	48	47	46
8	9	10	11	12	41	42	43	44	45
17	16	15	14	13	40	39	38	37	36
18	19	20	21	22	31	32	33	34	35
				23	30				
				24	29				
				25	28				
				26	27				

Intermediate Division - Patolli

For this program all of the marker moves will be by the player's marker at the lowest numbered location.

Using Sample #1, the 3 opponent's markers are at Locations #4, 14 and 24. The player's markers are at Locations #1, 8 and 12. There will be 6 die rolls. The first die roll is a 6. Being the lowest numbered marker, the marker at Location #1 moves to Location #7. 7 is a prime number. The marker should move 6 locations forward but is blocked at Location #8. It stays at Location #7. The next roll is a 3. The marker at Location #7 stops at Location #10. The lowest numbered player marker is at Location #8. The next die roll is a 5. The marker moves to Location #13. 13 is prime, so the marker should move 6 locations forward, but is blocked at 14. It stays at Location #13. The next die roll is a 1. The lowest player marker is at Location #10. The marker moves to
Location #11. 11 is a prime number so it tries to move forward 6 spaces, but is blocked by the player's marker at Location #12 so it stays at location #11. The lowest numbered player marker is a Location #11. The next die roll is a 5. It moves to Location #16 which is a perfect square so it tries to move 6 spaces backward, but is blocked at location #14 so it stops at Location #15. The last die roll is a 6 so it tries to move the marker at Location #12 to Location #18, but the move goes from at least 1 horizontal move (16 to 17) to at least 1 vertical move (17 to 18) so the marker must land on a multiple of 6. It stops at location #18.

INPUT: There will be 5 lines of input. Each line will contain the 3 values giving the locations of the opponent's markers on the board. That will be followed by the location of the 3 player's markers. That will be followed by an integer, r, giving the number of die rolls followed by the value of those die rolls.

OUTPUT: For each line of input, print the location numbers of the player's markers on the grid in numerical order. If there are no player's markers on the grid, print GAME OVER.

SAMPLE INPUT: http://www.datafiles.acsl.org/2020/contest4/int-sample-input.txt

4 14 24 1 8 12 6 6 3 5 1 5 6
14 28 31 10 20 24 7 6 6 5 5 6 2 4
5 30 33 3 20 24 8 6 6 6 5 6 3 4 6
4 11 15 2 8 20 5 5 2 5 1 6
45 50 48 42 46 40 6 3 2 6 5 4 1

SAMPLE OUTPUT:

1. 13 15 18
2. 26 29 30
3. 20 23 24
4. 14 16 20
5. 44 46 47

Intermediate Division - Patolli

TEST DATA

TEST INPUT:

37 41 47 35 43 48 6 5 5 6 5 4 2
13 29 39 15 21 31 10 4 5 2 4 6 6 5 5 6 5
43 47 40 28 30 32 10 5 3 2 6 1 5 2 6 3 2
1 5 10 2 12 8 12 5 5 4 4 3 3 2 2 1 1 6 6
20 25 15 30 18 24 16 6 6 4 5 2 1 6 4 2 3 6 5 4 5 3 1

TEST OUTPUT:

1. 49 50
2. 34 35 36
3. 37 38 39
4. 9 11 12
5. 32 33 35

American Computer Science League

2019-2020 Contest #4

JUNIOR DIVISION

1. Graph Theory

How many 1's are in the adjacency matrix for this directed graph?

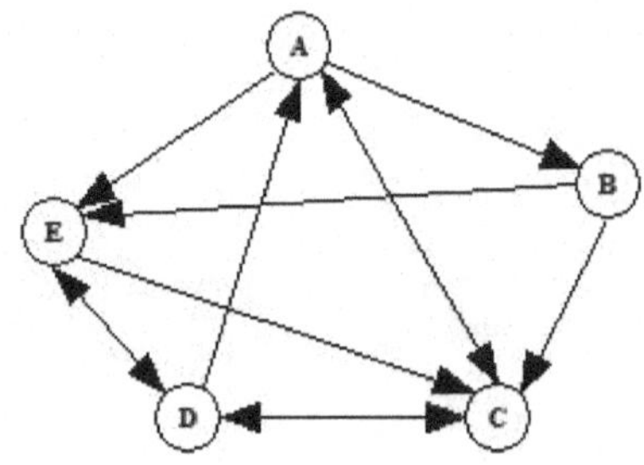

1.

2. Graph Theory

How many cycles are there from vertex A in the directed graph?

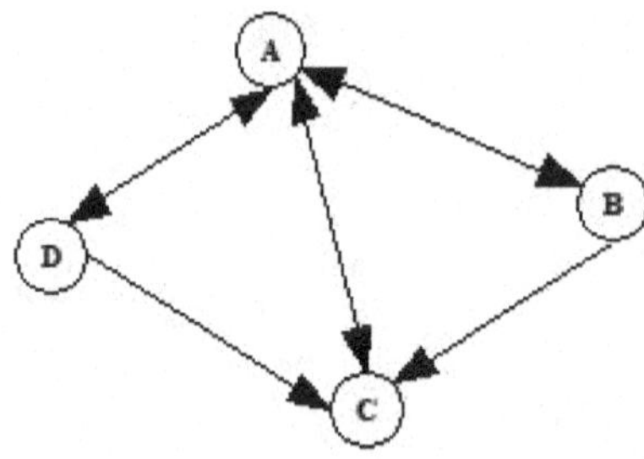

2.

3. Digital Electronics

Simplify the Boolean expression represented by the following digital circuit.

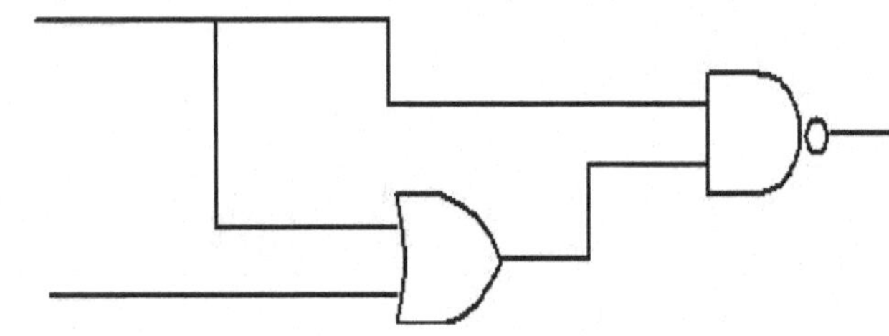

3.

4. Digital Electronics How many ordered quadruples make the following digital circuit TRUE?	4.

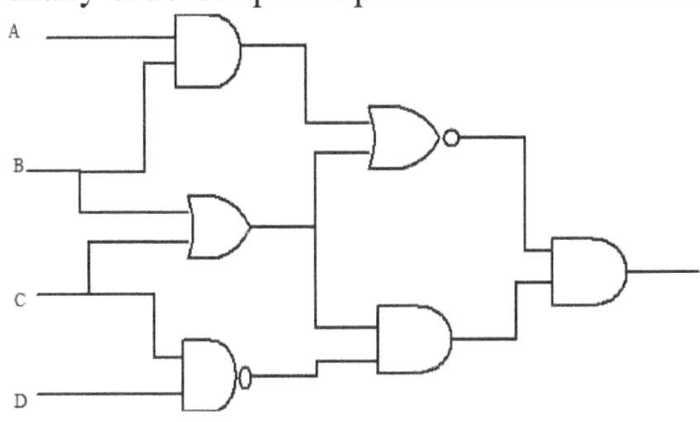

5. What Does This Program Do? - Strings — 5.

How many unique letters are in the output of the following program?

```
A = "HARTFORDISTHEINSURANCECAPITALOFTHEWORLD"
for i  = 0 to len(A) - 1
      if A[i] <= "H" then
          B = B + A[i]
      end if
      if A[i] >= "P" then
          C = C + A[i]
      end if
  next i
  for i  = 0 to len(B) - 1
       if B[i] != "A" && B[i] != "E" then
           D = D + B[i]
       end if
  next i
  for i = 0 to len(C) - 1
       if C[i] != "R" && C[i] != "T" then
           E = E + C[i]
       end if
  next i
  if len(D) <= len(E) then
        for i = 0 to len(D) - 1
            F = F + D[i] + E[i]
        next i
  else
        for i = 0 to len(E) - 1
            F = F + D[i] + E[i]
        next i
  end if
print F
end
```

American Computer Science League

2019-2020 Contest #4

JUNIOR DIVISION SOLUTIONS

1. Graph Theory

The adjacency matrix is :

0	1	1	0	1
0	0	1	0	1
1	0	0	1	0
1	0	1	0	1
0	0	1	1	0

1. 12

2. Graph Theory

The cycles are: ABA, ACA, ADA, ABCA, ADCA.

2. 5

3. Digital Electronics

The circuit translates to: $\overline{A(A+B)}$

$$\overline{A(A+B)}$$
$$= \overline{A} + \overline{(A+B)}$$
$$= \overline{A} + \overline{A}\,\overline{B}$$
$$= \overline{A}(1 + \overline{B})$$
$$= \overline{A}$$

3. $\overline{A}$
or NOT A
or ~A

American Computer Science League

2019-2020 — Contest #4

JUNIOR DIVISION SOLUTIONS

4. Digital Electronics

The circuit translates to:

$$\overline{A\,B + (B + C)}\ \ ((B + C)\,\overline{CD})$$

$$\overline{AB + (B+C)}((B+C)\,\overline{CD}) = 1$$
$$\Rightarrow \overline{AB+(B+C)} = 1 \wedge ((B+C)\,\overline{CD}) = 1$$
$$\Rightarrow (AB = 0 \wedge B+C = 0) \wedge (B+C=1 \wedge CD = 0)$$
$$\Rightarrow B+C = 0 \wedge B + C = 1 \textit{ which is impossible}.$$

Answer: 4. 0

5. What Does This Program Do? - Strings

A = “HARTFORDISTHEINSURANCECAPITALOFTHEWORLD”
The first loop forms B - letters alphabetically before I.
B = “HAFDHEACECAAFHED”
The second loop forms C - letters alphabetically after O.
C = “RTRSTSURPTTWR”
Drop A’s and E’s in B to form D = “HFDHCCFHD”.
Drop R’s and T’s in C to form E = “SSUPW”.
F is formed by alternating corresponding positions in D and E for the length of the shorter. F = “HSFSDUHPCW”.
There are 8 unique letters in F: H, S, F, D, U, P, C, W

Answer: 5. 8

2019-2020 **AMERICAN COMPUTER SCIENCE LEAGUE** Contest #4

Junior Division - Patolli

PROBLEM: Given the grid below for the game of ACSL Patolli, utilize the following rules to play the game. All rules must be applied in the sequential order listed.

1. There are 2 players. Each player has 3 markers.
2. The markers move according to the roll of a die (1 – 6).
3. Markers move in numerical order around the grid.
4. If, on a die roll, a marker lands on an occupied location, then that marker loses its turn and remains at its previous location.
5. A marker can jump over another marker on its way to finish its move.
6. A marker finishes its way around the grid when it lands on location 52. It is then removed from the board. A move can't take a marker beyond location 52. If it does, the marker remains at its previous location.
7. If, on a die roll, a marker lands on an unoccupied location that is a prime number, the marker then moves six locations forward. However, it stops immediately before any occupied location.
8. If, on a die roll, a marker lands on an unoccupied location that is a perfect square greater than 4, the marker then moves 6 locations backwards. However, it stops immediately before any occupied location.
9. If, on a die roll, a marker lands on an unoccupied location that is neither a prime number nor a perfect square, then determine if the marker made at least one horizontal move followed by at least one vertical move (such as going from 6 to 8, 11 to 13, 26 to 28 … but not 2 to 4 or 30 to 32). In that case, the marker can only land on a location on its path that is a multiple of the die roll value even if it moves a smaller distance than the die roll value. However, if all the locations in its path that are multiples are occupied, then the marker does not move from its current location. The rules listed in #7 and #8 do not apply when using #9.

				1	52				
				2	51				
7	6	5	4	3	50	49	48	47	46
8	9	10	11	12	41	42	43	44	45
17	16	15	14	13	40	39	38	37	36
18	19	20	21	22	31	32	33	34	35
				23	30				
				24	29				
				25	28				
				26	27				

Junior Division - Patolli

For this program, just one player marker will be moved.

Using Sample Input #1, locations 4, 6 and 8 contain an opponent's marker. The marker starting at Location #1 moves 6 spaces to Location #7. 7 is a prime so the marker should move to Location #13, but it is blocked by a marker at location 8. Therefore, it stays at location #7. It then moves 3 spaces to Location #10. The next die roll is a 5, but the move goes from at least 1 horizontal move (11 to 12) to at least 1 vertical move (12 to 13), so the marker must land on a multiple of 5 It stops at Location #15. The next die roll is a 1. The marker moves to Location #16. 16 is a perfect square and since there are no opponent's markers in the way, the marker can move 6 locations backwards to Location #10. The next die roll is a 1 and the marker moves to Location #11. 11 is a prime so the marker moves 6 locations forward to Location #17.

INPUT: There will be 5 lines of input. Each line will contain the 3 values giving the locations of the opponent's markers on the board. That will be followed by the location of the one player marker that will be moved. That will be followed by an integer, r, giving the number of die rolls followed by the value of those die rolls.

OUTPUT: For each line of input, print the final location number of the player's marker. If the marker lands on Location #52, print GAME OVER.

SAMPLE INPUT: http://www.datafiles.acsl.org/2020/contest4/jr-sample-input.txt

4 6 8 1 5 6 3 5 1 1
10 24 32 8 4 4 4 3 5
10 22 32 8 7 4 4 3 5 5 5 6
17 20 27 16 7 3 5 4 6 5 1 4
43 46 50 40 5 3 1 2 4 4

SAMPLE OUTPUT

1. 17
2. 23
3. 33
4. 34
5. GAME OVER

Junior Division - Patolli

TEST DATA

TEST INPUT:

25 27 49 22 7 2 2 6 6 5 3 6
50 41 38 45 9 4 2 5 3 1 6 4 3 1
21 26 30 19 6 6 4 6 1 2 3
5 14 18 2 7 2 5 4 5 2 1 6
10 17 20 9 12 4 5 3 1 6 2 3 3 5 4 1 6

TEST OUTPUT:

1. 42
2. GAME OVER
3. 27
4. 15
5. 48

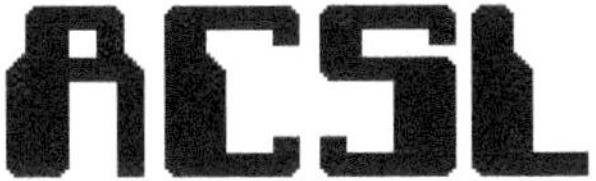

American Computer Science League

2019-2020 — Contest #4

ELEMENTARY DIVISION

1. Graph Theory Given the following description, list all of the edges represented using the first letter of each person's name. Do not include any duplicates. Amy shakes hands with Dave and Eli. Eli shakes hands with Amy and Ben. Ben shakes hands with Eli, Carol, and Dave. Dave shakes hands with Amy, Ben, and Carol. Carol shakes hands with Ben and Dave.	1.
2. Graph Theory For the given graph, identify the set of edges needed for this graph to be a complete graph. List them in alphabetical order (AB, not BA). 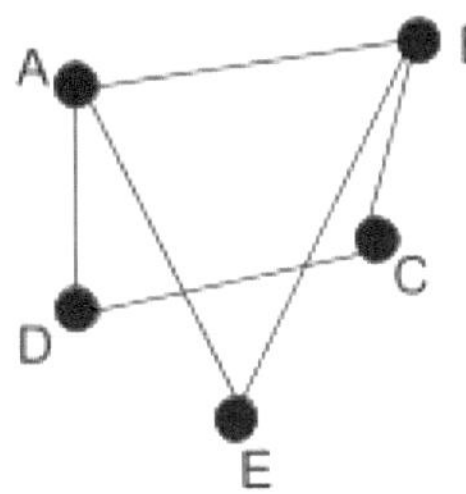	2.
3. Graph Theory If you are delivering pizza from location Q to all other places and returning to location Q when you are finished, how many different routes could you take? (In order words, count the number of Hamiltonian circuits starting with vertex Q.) 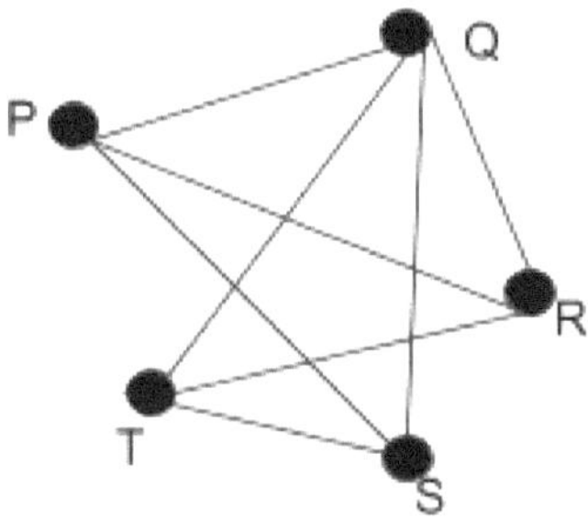	3.

American Computer Science League

2019-2020 — **Contest #4**

ELEMENTARY DIVISION

4. Graph Theory

In the undirected graph shown below, how many cycles are there? Remember that cycles must include at least 3 vertices in an undirected graph and it is a different cycle if it goes the opposite way.

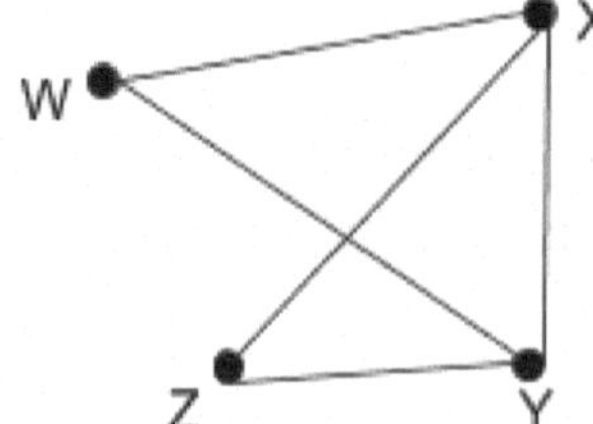

4.

5. Graph Theory

Identify the starting and ending vertices that must be used in order to traverse the following graph. If it is not possible, write NONE.

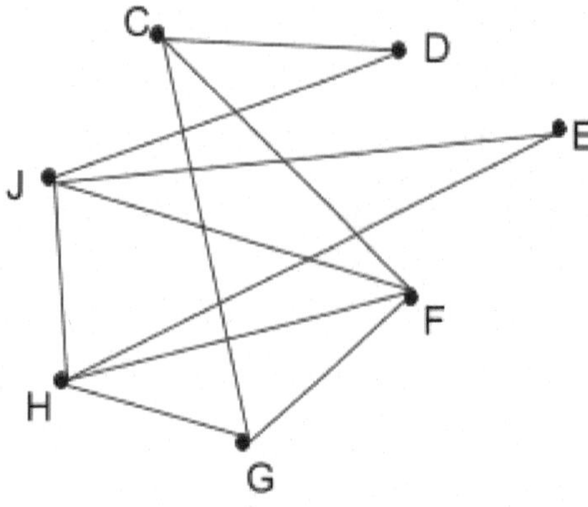

5.

American Computer Science League

2019-2020 — Contest #4

ELEMENTARY DIVISION SOLUTIONS

1. Graph Theory There are 6 edges that should be listed. The answer is as shown.	**1.** AD, AE, BC, BD, BE, CD (They may be listed in any order and letters may be reversed.)
2. Graph Theory A complete graph includes an edge from every vertex to every other vertex. That means that there should be 4+3+2+1=10 edges. The current graph has 6 edges so 4 more are needed. They are listed.	**2.** AC, BD, CE, DE (They may be listed in any order, but the letters may not be reversed.)
3. Graph Theory By inspection, the Hamiltonian circuits starting with Q are: QRPSTQ or QTSPRQ, QRTSPQ or QPSTRQ, QPRTSQ or QSTRPQ, and QTRPSQ or QSPRTQ, There are 4 pair so a total of **8** of them.	**3.** 8
4. Graph Theory By inspection, there are 4 of length 3 going both ways: WXYW, WYXW, XYZX, XZYX. There are 2 of length 4 going both ways: WXZYW and WYZXW. There are a total of **6** of them. The number of cycles should always be an even number.	**4.** 6
5. Graph Theory Traversable graphs must have an even number of vertices that each have an odd number of edges connected to it. The only vertices with an odd number of edges connected to them are C and G. 2 is even. .	**5.** C and G (in either order)

American Computer Science League

2019-2020 Contest #4

CLASSROOM DIVISION

1. Graph Theory How many 1's are in the adjacency matrix for this directed graph? 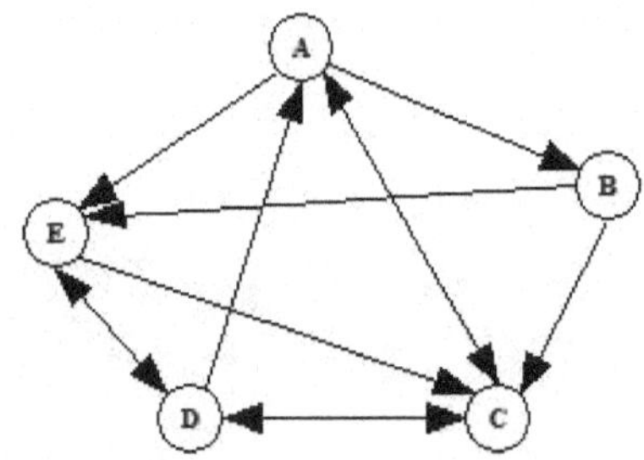 	1.
2. Graph Theory How many cycles are there from vertex A in the directed graph? 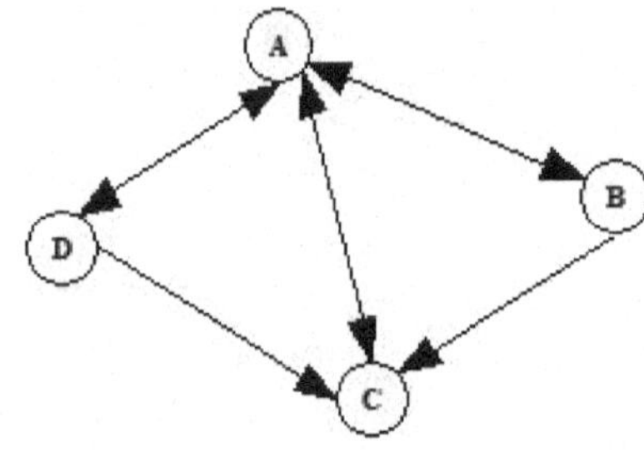 	2.
3. Digital Electronics Simplify the Boolean expression represented by the following digital circuit. 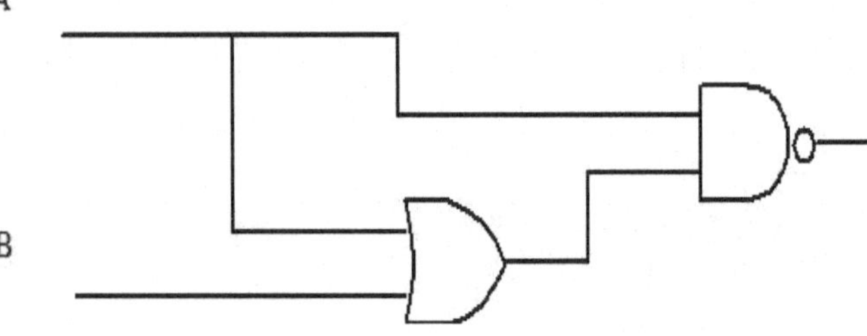 	3.

4. Digital Electronics

4.

How many ordered quadruples make the following digital circuit TRUE?

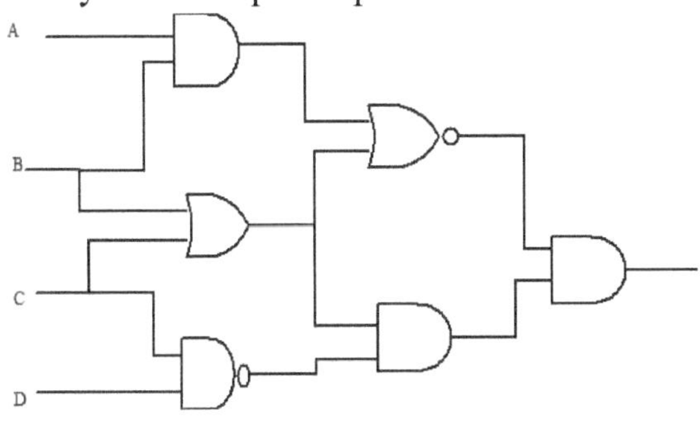

5. What Does This Program Do? - Strings

5.

How many unique letters are in the output of the following program?

```
A = "HARTFORDISTHEINSURANCECAPITALOFTHEWORLD"
for i  = 0 to len(A) - 1
      if A[i] <= "H" then
          B = B + A[i]
      end if
      if A[i] >= "P" then
          C = C + A[i]
      end if
 next i
 for i  = 0 to len(B) - 1
      if B[i] != "A" && B[i] != "E" then
          D = D + B[i]
      end if
 next i
 for i = 0 to len(C) - 1
      if C[i] != "R" && C[i] != "T" then
          E = E + C[i]
      end if
 next i
 if len(D) <= len(E) then
       for i = 0 to len(D) - 1
           F = F + D[i] + E[i]
       next i
 else
       for i = 0 to len(E) - 1
           F = F + D[i] + E[i]
       next i
 end if
print F
end
```

American Computer Science League

2019-2020 — Contest #4

CLASSROOM DIVISION

6. Graph Theory — 6.

After drawing the following directed graph, how many pairs of different vertices have no edge in either direction between them?

Vertices: {A, B ,C, D, E, F} and
Edges: {AB, FD, CC, EA, FE, AC, DB, FA, CB, EE, BD}

7. Graph Theory — 7.

How many more paths of length 3 are there than of length 2 in this directed graph?

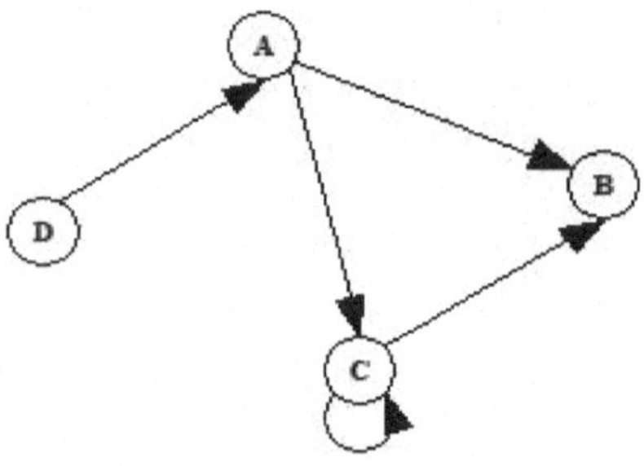

8. Digital Electronics — 8.

Simplify the Boolean expression represented by the following digital circuit. Perform all indicated operations.

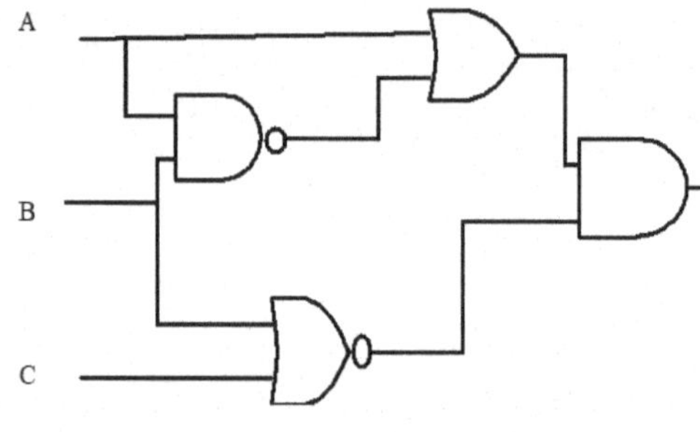

9. Digital Electronics

9.

How many ordered triples make the Boolean expression represented by this digital circuit TRUE?

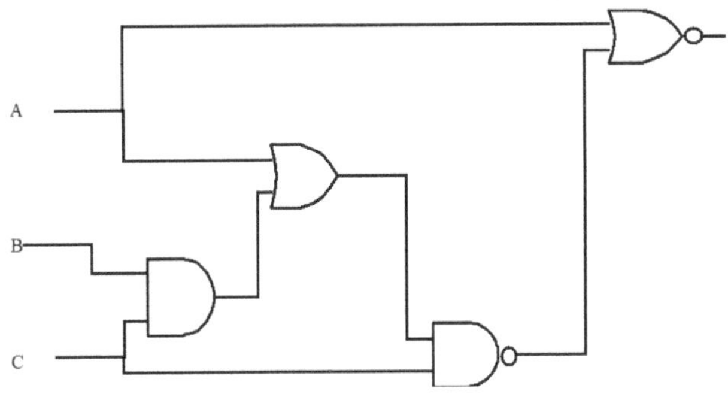

10. Assembly Language

10.

What is output when this program is executed?

```
        X   DC    8
        Y   DC    15
TOP     LOAD      X
        MULT      X
        SUB       Y
        BL        L
        LOAD      X
        SUB       =1
        STORE     X
        LOAD      Y
        SUB       =1
        STORE     Y
        BU        TOP
L       PRINT     X
        END
```

American Computer Science League

2019-2020 **Contest #4**

CLASSROOM DIVISION SOLUTIONS

1. Graph Theory

The adjacency matrix is :

0	1	1	0	1
0	0	1	0	1
1	0	0	1	0
1	0	1	0	1
0	0	1	1	0

1. 12

2. Graph Theory

The cycles are: ABA, ACA, ADA, ABCA, ADCA.

2. 5

3. Digital Electronics

The circuit translates to: $\overline{A(A+B)}$

$$\overline{A(A+B)}$$
$$= \overline{A} + \overline{(A+B)}$$
$$= \overline{A} + \overline{A}\,\overline{B}$$
$$= \overline{A}(1 + \overline{B})$$
$$= \overline{A}$$

3. $\overline{A}$
or NOT A
or ~A

American Computer Science League

2019-2020 **Contest #4**

CLASSROOM DIVISION SOLUTIONS

4. Digital Electronics

4. 0

The circuit translates to:

$$\overline{A\,B + (B + C)}\ \ (\ (B + C)\ \overline{CD})$$

$$\overline{AB + (B+C)}\,(\,(B+C)\,\overline{CD}) = 1$$

$$\Rightarrow \overline{AB + (B+C)} = 1 \wedge (\,(B+C)\,\overline{CD}) = 1$$

$$\Rightarrow (AB = 0 \wedge B+C = 0) \wedge (B+C=1 \wedge CD = 0)$$

$$\Rightarrow B+C = 0 \wedge B + C = 1 \textit{ which is impossible}.$$

5. What Does This Program Do? - Strings

5. 8

A = "HARTFORDISTHEINSURANCECAPITALOFTHEWORLD"
The first loop forms B - letters alphabetically before I.
B = "HAFDHEACECAAFHED"
The second loop forms C - letters alphabetically after O.
C = "RTRSTSURPTTWR"
Drop A's and E's in B to form D = "HFDHCCFHD".
Drop R's and T's in C to form E = "SSUPW".
F is formed by alternating corresponding positions in D and E for the length of the shorter. F = "HSFSDUHPCW".
There are 8 unique letters in F: H, S, F, D, U, P, C, W

American Computer Science League

2019-2020 Contest #4

CLASSROOM DIVISION SOLUTIONS

6. Graph Theory There are 7 different pairs of vertices with no direct edge between them: 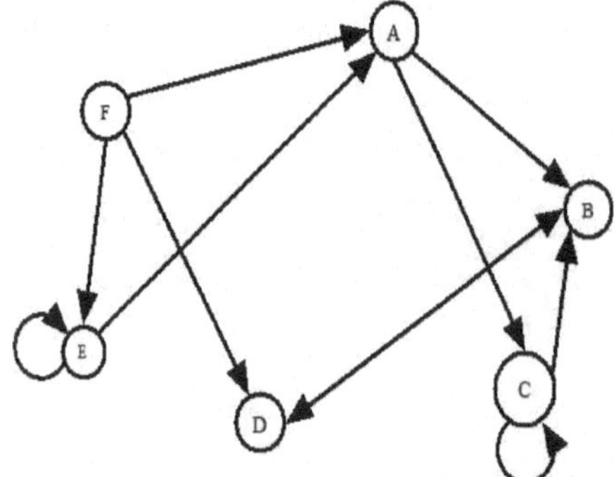 AD, BE, BF, CD, CE, CF, and DE.	**6.** 7
7. Graph Theory $M=\begin{bmatrix}0&1&1&0\\0&0&0&0\\0&1&1&0\\1&0&0&0\end{bmatrix}$ $M^2=\begin{bmatrix}0&1&1&0\\0&0&0&0\\0&1&1&0\\0&1&1&0\end{bmatrix}$ $M^3=\begin{bmatrix}0&1&1&0\\0&0&0&0\\0&1&1&0\\0&1&1&0\end{bmatrix}$ There are 6 paths of length 2 and 6 paths of length 3. The difference is 0.	**7.** 0
8. Digital Electronics The digital circuit translates to: $(A + \overline{AB})\left(\overline{B + C}\right)$ $= (A + \overline{A} + \overline{B})\ \overline{B}\,\overline{C}$ $= \left(1 + \overline{B}\right)\overline{B}\,\overline{C}$ $= \overline{B}\,\overline{C}$	**8.** $\overline{B}\,\overline{C}$ or $\overline{B+C}$ Either answer is accepted.

9. Digital Electronics

The digital circuit translates to:

$$\overline{A + \overline{(A + BC)\,C}}$$
$$= \overline{A}(A + BC)\,C$$
$$= \overline{A}AC + \overline{A}BC$$
$$= 0 + \overline{A}BC$$
$$= \overline{A}BC$$

So (0,1,1) makes it TRUE.

9. 1

10. Assembly Language

An equivalent program using our WDTPD language is:

```
X = 8
Y = 15
while X * X - Y >= 0
   X = X - 1
   Y = Y - 1
end while
output X
```

X	8	7	6	5	4	3
Y	15	14	13	12	11	10
X*X-Y	49	35	23	13	5	-1

10. 3

Finals

American Computer Science League

2020 Finals • Shorts Problems • Senior Division

1. Boolean Algebra

Simplify the following Boolean expression to use AND, OR, and NOT operators with no parentheses. How many OR operators are there?

$$\overline{A+\overline{B}C} + \overline{B+\overline{AC}} + \overline{\overline{C}+AB}$$

A. 0
B. 1
C. 2
D. 3
E. None of the above

2. Boolean Algebra

Define a new binary operator, $, as follows:

$$A \$ B = (A \oplus \overline{B})(\overline{A} \oplus B)$$

It has the highest priority among binary operators.

How many ordered triples make the following TRUE?

$$\overline{A} + A \cdot B \$ C$$

A. 0
B. 4
C. 6
D. 8
E. None of the above

3. Bit-String Flicking

Evaluate the following expression. Your answer must be written as a 3-digit base 16 number in the form *xyz* where each digit is 0-9 or A-F.

((NOT (RCIRC-7 $AB9_{16}$)) XOR (RSHIFT-3 ($CE9_{16}$ AND 915_{16})))

A. 2722
B. 9CA
C. 0CB
D. 4712
E. None of the above

4. Bit-String Flicking

How many different values of x (a bitstring of 5 bits) make the following equation true?

```
((RCIRC-2 (X AND 11011)) OR (RCIRC-2 X) XOR 01110)=
                (NOT (LSHIFT-4 01011))
```

A. 0
B. 2
C. 4
D. 8
E. None of the above

5. Recursive Functions

Find $f(14,20)$ given:

$$f(x,y) = \begin{cases} f(x+1, y-2) + f(y,x) + 1 & \text{if } x < y \\ f\left(f\left(x/2, y\right), x/2\right) - 3 & \text{if } x = y \\ x - y & \text{if } x > y \end{cases}$$

A. 19
B. 18
C. 11
D. 10
F. None of the above

6. Recursive Functions

My favorite Oak tree has a trunk that is 128 feet tall. It has 2 branches, each half that length. Each of those branches has 2 branches that are each half the length. If this continues until each branch is 1 foot long, how many total feet of branches is in the entire tree.

A. 512
B. 1024
C. 2048
D. 4096
E. None of the above

7. Digital Electronics

Find all ordered triples that make the following circuit TRUE. Your answer will be a single 3-character string in the format XYZ where each X Y Z is either 0, 1, or * (e.g. 0*1, 110, **0).

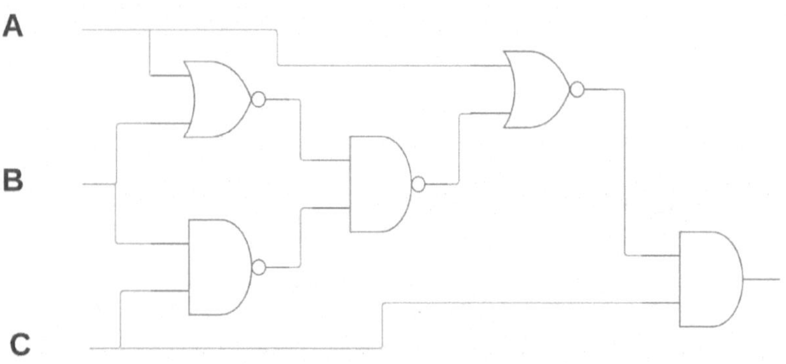

A. *01
B. 100
C. 0*0
D. 001
E. None of the above

8. Digital Electronics

Define a new gate , ☐ , with 3 inputs. It is TRUE if there is exactly one TRUE input. How many ordered triples make the following digital circuit TRUE?

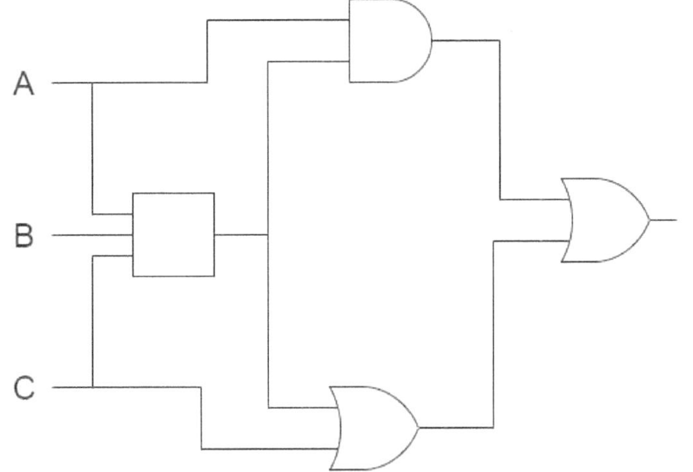

A. 0
B. 2
C. 4
D. 6
E. None of the above

9. Prefix-Infix-Postfix

Define M(x,y,z) as a trinary function that returns the smallest value of the three operands, A(x,y) as a binary function that finds the average of the two operands, and R(x) as the reciprocal of its operand.

Evaluate the following postfix expression (all numbers are single digits):

```
3 5 - 0 4 M 4 2 A 6 R * * 8 5 3 4 + M 3 A / R
```

A. -4
B. 1
C. 3
D. 4
E. None of the above

10. Prefix-Infix-Postfix

Evaluate this prefix expression if a = 1, b=3, c=5, and d=2:

```
+ * d ^ b - b c / * a - + b c a ^ b d
```

A. 9
B. 6
C. 3
D. 1
E. None of the above

11. Computer Number Systems

Evaluate and express the result in decimal:

$$\mathbf{2020_{16} - 2020_{10} - 2020_{8}}$$

A. 5148
B. 5164
C. 5224
D. 11284
E. None of the above

12. Computer Number Systems

How many 1's are in the binary representation of the following expression:

$$\mathbf{(AB_{16} + DA_{16}) * 77_{8}}$$

A. 10
B. 11
C. 12
D. 13
E. None of the above

13. Data Structures

Perform the following operations on an initially empty queue:

PUSH(C), PUSH(H), PUSH(R), PUSH(Y), POP(X), POP(X),
PUSH(S), POP(X), PUSH(A), PUSH(N), PUSH(T), POP(X),
PUSH(H), PUSH(E), POP(X), POP(X), PUSH(M), PUSH(U),
POP(X), PUSH(M), POP(X), POP(X)

What is the most number of items in the queue at any time?

A. 7
B. 6
C. 5
D. 4
E. None of the above

14. Data Structures

How many nodes have only one child in the binary search tree for:

`PROTECTIVEEQUIPMENT`

A. 2
B. 4
C. 6
D. 9
E. None of the above

15. Graph Theory

How many cycles are there in the directed graph represented by the following adjacency matrix?

$$\begin{bmatrix} 1 & 0 & 0 & 1 & 1 \\ 0 & 0 & 1 & 1 & 0 \\ 1 & 0 & 0 & 1 & 0 \\ 0 & 1 & 0 & 1 & 1 \\ 0 & 0 & 1 & 0 & 1 \end{bmatrix}$$

A. 10
B. 9
C. 8
D. 7
E. None of the above

6. Graph Theory

How many pairs of vertices have more than 7 paths of length 4 between them?

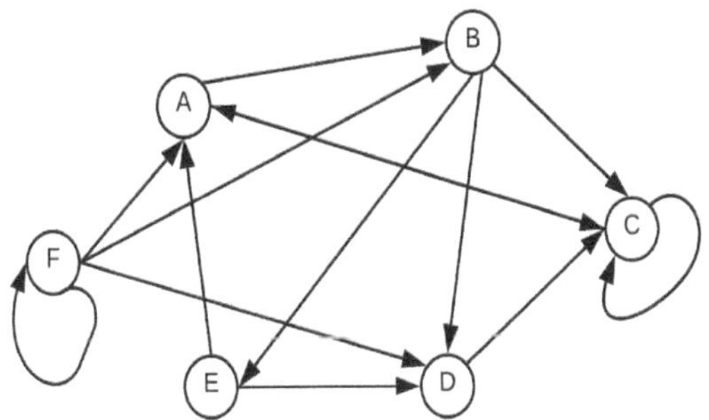

A. 5
B. 6
C. 7
D. 8
E. None of the above

17. What Does This Program Do?

What will be printed when the following program is run?

```
Y = 2020 : S = 0 : N = 0 : F = 0
for A = 1 to Y
   if Y % A == 0 then
       S = S + A
       N = N + 1
   end if
   if S > Y and F = 0 then
       output N - 1
       F = 1
   end if
next
```

A. 8
B. 9
C. 10
D. 11
E. None of the above

18. LISP

After the following LISP program is run, what is the value of the CONS expression?

```
(SETQ Z '(C (O N) (N (E C) T) (I (C (U) T))))
(SETQ S (CDR (CDR Z)))
(SETQ Y (CAR (REVERSE S)))
(SETQ X (CAR (CDR (CAR (CDR Y)))))
(SETQ V (CAR (CDR (CAR S))))
(CONS V X)
```

A. (E C U)
B. ((E C) U)
C. ((E C) (U))
D. (E C (U))
E. None of the above

19. FSAs and Regular Expressions

Given the regular expression:

```
[^aeiou]*[aeiou][fghj-np-t]+.(ing|ful|age|less)?
```

Identify all of the following strings that are accepted.

```
a. brush|ing      f. shapeless      k. grapple
b. help/ful       g. igloo          l. rhythmic?
c. fractals       h. apple          m. allstar
d. java           i. striving       n. syzygy
e. python!        j. image          o. covid
```

A. a, b, d. e, f, g
B. a, c, d , e, l
C. b, c, d, g, h. n. o
D. a, b, e, f, h, k
E. None of the above

20. Assembly Language

How many different numbers are printed when the following program is run with input values 13, 24, 37, 45, 51, 60, 74, 0?

```
TOP     READ    N
        LOAD    N
        BE      STOP
        DIV     =10
        STORE   B
        MULT    =10
        STORE   X
        LOAD    N
        SUB     X
        STORE   C
        LOAD    B
        ADD     C
        STORE   M
        DIV     =3
        MULT    =3
        STORE   Y
        LOAD    M
        SUB     Y
        BE      DOWN
        BU      TOP
DOWN    LOAD    N
        PRINT   N
        BU      TOP
STOP    END
```

A. 4
B. 3
C. 2
D. 1
E. None of the above

American Computer Science League

2020 Finals • Solutions to Short Problems • Senior Division

1. Boolean Algebra

$$\overline{A + \overline{B}C} + \overline{B + \overline{AC}} + \overline{\overline{C} + AB}$$

$$= \overline{A}\,\overline{\overline{B}C} + \overline{B}\,\overline{\overline{AC}} + \overline{\overline{C}}\,\overline{AB}$$

$$= \overline{A}(\overline{\overline{B}} + \overline{C}) + \overline{B}AC + \overline{\overline{C}}(\overline{A} + \overline{B})$$

$$= \overline{A}B + \overline{A}\,\overline{C} + \overline{B}AC + \overline{A}C + \overline{B}C$$

$$= \overline{A}B + \overline{A}(\overline{C} + C) + A\overline{B}C + \overline{B}C$$

$$= \overline{A}B + \overline{A} + \overline{B}C(A + 1)$$

$$= \overline{A}B + \overline{A} + \overline{B}C$$

$$= \overline{A}(B + 1) + \overline{B}C$$

$$= \overline{A} + \overline{B}C$$

There is one OR operator.

1. 1 (B)

2. Boolean Algebra

$A \$ B = (A \oplus \overline{B})(\overline{A} \oplus B)$ simplified is $AB + \overline{A}\,\overline{B}$.

Therefore, $\overline{A} + A \cdot B \$ C$
$= \overline{A} + A(BC + \overline{B}\,\overline{C})$
$= \overline{A} + ABC + A\overline{B}\,\overline{C}$.

$\overline{A}$ is TRUE for the ordered triples (0,*,*) and the other two ordered triples are (1,1,1) and (1,0,0) so there are a total of 6.

2. 6 (C)

3. Bit-String Flicking

Change all to binary:

$AB9_{16}$ = 101010111001, $CE9_{16}$ = 110011101001,
915_{16} = 100100010101

((NOT (RCIRC-7 $AB9_{16}$)) XOR (RSHIFT-3 ($CE9_{16}$ AND 915_{16})))
= ((NOT (RCIRC-7 101010111001)) XOR
(RSHIFT-3 (110011101001 AND 100100010101)))
= ((NOT 011100110101) XOR (RSHIFT-3 100000000001))
= 1000 1100 1010 XOR 0001 0000 0000
= 1001 1100 1010
= 9 C A

3. 9CA (B)

4. Bit-String Flicking Let X = abcde and NOT X = ABCDE ((RCIRC-2 (X AND 11011)) OR (RCIRC-2 X) XOR 01110)= (NOT (LSHIFT-4 01011)) ((RCIRC-2 (abcde AND 11011)) OR (RCIRC-2 abcde) XOR 01110) = (RCIRC-2 ab0de) OR (deabc XOR 01110) because XOR has a higher priority than OR does. LHS: deab0 OR dEABc RHS: (NOT (LSHIFT-4 01011)) = NOT 10000 = 01111. Therefore, d + d = 0 so d = 0, e + E = 1 which is always TRUE, a + A = 1 which is always TRUE, b + B = which is always TRUE, and 0 + c = 1 so c = 1. which gives the bit string solution **10* so there are 8 solutions.	4. 8 (D)
5. Recursive Functions $f(14,20) = f(14+1,20-2) + f(14,20) + 1$ $= f(15,18) + f(20,14) + 1 = 12 + 6 + 1 = 19$ $f(15,18) = f(15+1,18-2) + f(18,15) + 1$ $= f(16,16) + f(18,15) + 1 = 8 + 3 + 1 = 12$ $f(20,14) = 20 - 14 = 6$ $f(16,16) = f\left(f\left(\frac{16}{2},16\right),\frac{16}{2}\right) - 3 = f(f(8,16),8) - 3$ $= f(19,8) - 3 = 11 - 3 = 8$ $f(18,15) = 18 - 15 = 3$ $f(8,16) = f(8+1,16-2) + f(16,8) + 1$ $= f(9,14) + f(16,8) + 1 = 10 + 8 + 1 = 19$ $f(9,14) = f(9+1,14-2) + f(14,9) + 1$ $= f(10,12) + f(14,9) + 1 = 4 + 5 + 1 = 10$ $f(16,8) = 16 - 8 = 8$ $f(14,9) = 14 - 9 = 5$ $f(10,12) = f(10+1,12-2) + f(12,10) + 1$ $= f(11,10) + f(12,10) + 1 = 1 + 2 + 1 = 4$ $f(11,10) = 11 - 10 = 1$ $f(12,10) = 12 - 10 = 2$ $f(19,8) = 19 - 8 = 11$	5. 19 (A)

6. Recursive Functions

The pattern is that there is 1 trunk of length 128; there are 2 branches of length 64; there are 4 branches of length 32; there are 8 branches of length 16; there are 16 branches of length 8; there are 32 branches of length 4; there are 64 branches of length 2; and there are 128 branches of length 1. Each product is 128 and there are 8 of them. 128 x 8 = 1024 for a total length of all branches on the tree.

6. 1024 (B)

7. Digital Electronics

The digital circuit translates to:

$$\overline{(A + \overline{\overline{(A + B)}\,\overline{(B\,C)}})}\ C$$

$$= \overline{A}\,\overline{\overline{\overline{(A + B)}\,\overline{(B\,C)}}}\,C$$

$$= \overline{A}\ \overline{(A + B)}\,\overline{(B\,C)}\,C$$

$$= \overline{A}\ (\overline{A}\,\overline{B})(\overline{B} + \overline{C})\,C$$

$$= \overline{A}\,\overline{B}\ (\overline{B} + \overline{C})\,C$$

$$= \overline{A}\,\overline{B}\,C + \overline{A}\,\overline{B}\,\overline{C}\,C$$

$= \overline{A}\ \overline{B}\ C$ which is TRUE if A = 0, B=0, and C=1.

7. 001 (D)

8. Digital Electronics

The circuit translates to: (A)(□(A, B, C) + ((□(A, B, C) + C)

Let X = □ (A, B, C) The expression is now: A X + (X + C)

A	B	C	X	AX	X + C	AX + (X+C)
0	0	0	0	0	0	0
0	0	1	1	0	1	1
0	1	0	1	0	1	1
0	1	1	0	0	1	1
1	0	0	1	1	1	1
1	0	1	0	0	1	1
1	1	0	0	0	0	0
1	1	1	0	0	1	1

Therefore there are 6 triples that make the expression TRUE.

8. 6 (D)

9. Prefix-Infix-Postfix 3 5 - 0 4 M 4 2 A 6 R * * 8 5 3 4 + M 3 A / R = (3 5 -) 0 4 M (4 2 A) (6 R) * * 8 5 (3 4 +) M 3 A / R = (((-2 0 4 M) (3 1/6 *) *) ((8 5 7 M) 3 A) /) R = ((-2 1/2 *) (5 3 A) /) R =(-1 4 /) R = -1/4 R = -4	9. -4 (A)
10. Prefix-Infix-Postfix + * 2 ^ 3 - 3 5 / * 1 - + 3 5 1 ^ 3 2 = + * 2 ^ 3 (- 3 5) / * 1 - (+3 5) 1 (^ 3 2) = + * 2 (^ 3 -2) / * 1 (- 8 1) 9 = + (* 2 1/9) / (* 1 7) 9 = + 2/9 (/ 7 9) = (+ 2/9 7/9) = 1	10. 1 (D)
11. Computer Number Systems **2020_{16} - 2020_{10} - 2020_8** $2020_{16} = 2 * 16^3 + 2 * 16 = 2 * 2^{12} + 32 = 2^{13} + 32 = 8192 + 32$ $= 8224_{10}$ $2020_8 = 2 * 8^3 + 2 * 8 = 2 * 2^9 + 16 = 2^{10} + 16 = 1024 + 16 = 1040_{10}$ $8224_{10} - 2020_{10} = 6204_{10} - 1040_{10} = 5164_{10}$	11. 5164 (B)
12. Computer Number Systems $AB_{16} + DA_{16} = 185_{16} = 1\ 1000\ 0101_2 = 110\ 000\ 101_2 = 605_8$ $605_8 * 77_8 = 605_8 * (100_8 - 1_8) = 60500_8 - 605_8 = 57673_8$ $101\ 111\ 110\ 111\ 011_2$ which is 12 1's.	12. 12 (C)
13. Data Structures The queue looks like C H R Y. Pop the C, then the H. R Y S. Pop the R. Y S A N T. Pop the Y. S A N T H E. Pop the S and the A. N T H E M U. Pop the N. T H E M U M. Pop the T and the H. The longest length of the queue at any point in time is 6.	13. 6 (B)

14. Data Structures The binary search tree is drawn below. C, E, E, M, T, and V have only 1 child so there are 6 of them. 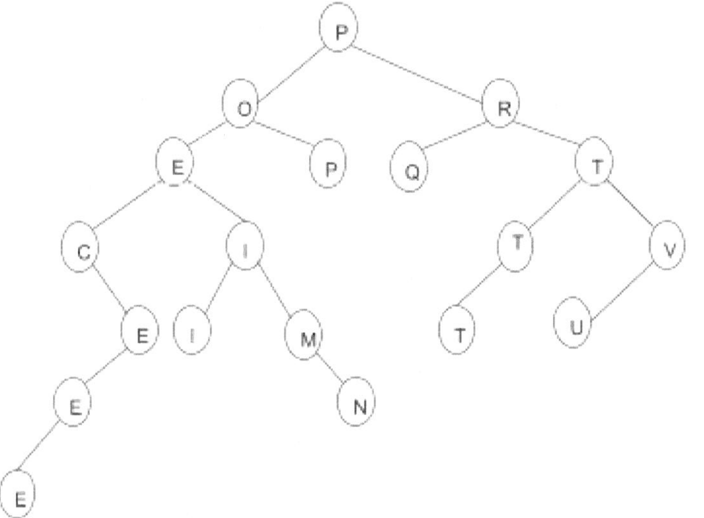	14. 6 (C)
15. Graph Theory The graph from the adjacency matrix is below. By inspection, the cycles are: AA, DD, EE, BDB, AECA, ADBCA, ADECA, BCDB, and CDEC. There are 9 of them. 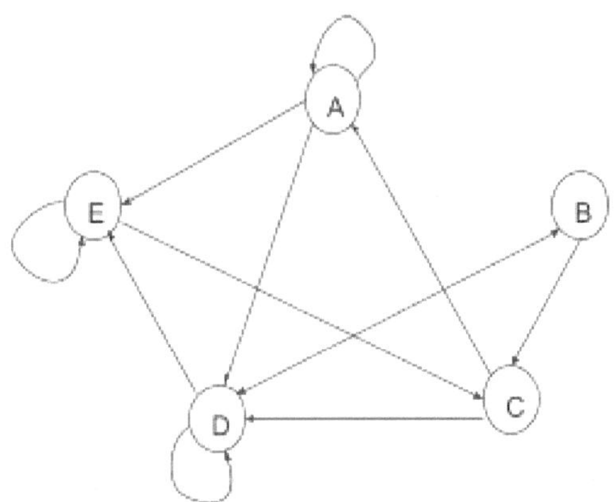	15. 9 (B)

16. Graph Theory	

To find the number of paths of length 4, find the adjacency matrix, square it for paths of length 2, and square that for paths of length 4. By inspection, there are 5 values that are greater than 7.

$$\begin{bmatrix} 0 & 1 & 1 & 0 & 0 & 0 \\ 0 & 0 & 1 & 1 & 1 & 0 \\ 1 & 0 & 1 & 0 & 0 & 0 \\ 0 & 0 & 1 & 0 & 0 & 0 \\ 1 & 0 & 0 & 1 & 0 & 0 \\ 1 & 1 & 0 & 1 & 0 & 1 \end{bmatrix}^2 = \begin{bmatrix} 1 & 0 & 2 & 1 & 1 & 0 \\ 2 & 0 & 2 & 1 & 0 & 0 \\ 1 & 1 & 2 & 0 & 0 & 0 \\ 1 & 0 & 1 & 0 & 0 & 0 \\ 0 & 1 & 2 & 0 & 0 & 0 \\ 1 & 2 & 3 & 2 & 1 & 1 \end{bmatrix}^2 = \begin{bmatrix} 4 & 3 & 9 & 1 & 1 & 0 \\ 5 & 2 & 9 & 2 & 2 & 0 \\ 5 & 2 & 8 & 2 & 1 & 0 \\ 2 & 1 & 4 & 1 & 1 & 0 \\ 4 & 2 & 6 & 1 & 0 & 0 \\ 11 & 6 & 19 & 5 & 2 & 1 \end{bmatrix}$$

16. 5 (A)

17. What Does This Program Do?

This program calculates the sum of the increasing factors of 2020 until that sum is more than 2020. They are 1, 2, 4, 5, 10, 20, 101, 202, 404 and 505.

17. 10 (C)

18. LISP Programming

If Z = '(C (O N) (N (E C) T) (I (C (U) T))),
S = '((N (E C) T) (I (C (U) T)))

Y = (CAR (REVERSE S)))
= (I (C (U) T))

X = (CAR (CDR '(C (U) T)))
= (CAR '((U) T))
= (U)

V = (CAR (CDR (CAR S)))
= (CAR (CDR '(N (E C) T))))
= (CAR '((E C) T))
= (E C)

(CONS V X) = ((E C) U)

18. ((E C) U) (B)

19. FSAs and Regular Expressions `[^aeiou]* [aeiou] [fghj-np-t] +. (ing|ful|age|less)?` a. brush|ing - OK b. help/ful - OK c. fractals - fails at C d. java - fails at V e. python! - OK f. shapeless - OK g. igloo - fails at second o h. apple - OK i. striving - fails at v j. image - fails at g k. grapple - OK l. rhythmic? - fails at c m. allstar - fails at second a n. syzygy - fails at end - no vowel o. covid - fails at v Therefore 6 of the choices satisfy the regular expression.	19. a, b, e, f, h, k (D)

20. Assembly Language
The assembly programs can be converted to ACSL WDTPD code as follows:
input n
while n != 0
  b = int(n / 10)
  x = b * 10
  c = n - x
  m = b + c
  y = m % 3
  if m == y then
    print n
  end if
  input n
end while
This program checks if a given number is divisible by 3 by adding the digits to see if the sum is a multiple of 3. There are 4 such numbers before inputting 0: 24, 45, 51, 60.
	20. 4 (A)

American Computer Science League

2020 Finals • Short Problems • Intermediate and Classroom Divisions

1. Boolean Algebra

Simplify the following Boolean expression to use AND, OR, and NOT operators with no parentheses. How many OR operators are there?

$$\overline{A+\overline{B}C}+\overline{B+\overline{AC}}+\overline{\overline{C}+AB}$$

A. 0
B. 1
C. 2
D. 3
E. None of the above

2. Boolean Algebra

Define a new operator, \$, as follows: $A \,\$\, B = \overline{A\,\overline{B}+\overline{A}}$

It has the highest precedence among binary operators.

How many ordered triples make the following FALSE?

$$A \,\$\, B + B \,\$\, C + \overline{A} \,\$\, \overline{C}$$

A. 0
B. 1
C. 3
D. 5
E. None of the above

3. Bit-String Flicking

Evaluate the following bit string expression if

X = 01101 and Y = 10110.

```
(RSHIFT-1 (LCIRC-3 X)) OR
(NOT (LSHIFT-1 ((RCIRC-2 X) & Y)))
```

A. 11111
B. 00101
C. 01101
D. 00000
E. None of the above

4. Bit-String Flicking

How many different values of x (a bitstring of 5 bits) make the following equation true?

```
(LCIRC-2 01010) OR
(RSHIFT-1 ((LCIRC-2 X) AND 01110))
= 01101
```

A. 0
B. 4
C. 8
D. 10
E. None of the above

5. Recursive Functions

Find $f(f(f(f(30))))$ where $[x]$ is the greatest integer function:

$$f(x) = \begin{cases} 2 \cdot f\left(\left[{}^{x}/_{2}\right]\right) - 3 & \text{if } x \text{ is odd and } x \text{ is a multiple of } 3 \\ f(x+3) + 1 & \text{if } x \text{ is even and } x \text{ is a multiple of } 3 \\ x - 1 & \text{otherwise} \end{cases}$$

A. 22
B. 21
C. 15
D. 9
E. None of the above

6. Recursive Functions

Find $f(14, 20)$ given:

$$f(x,y) = \begin{cases} f(x+1, y-2) + f(y,x) + 1 & \text{if } x < y \\ f\left(f\left({}^{x}/_{2}, y\right), {}^{x}/_{2}\right) - 3 & \text{if } x = y \\ x - y & \text{if } x > y \end{cases}$$

A. 19
B. 18
C. 11
D. 10
E. None of the above

7. Digital Electronics

Find all ordered triples that make the following circuit TRUE. Your answer will be a single 3-character string in the format XYZ where each X Y Z is either 0, 1, or * (e.g. 0*1, 110, **0).

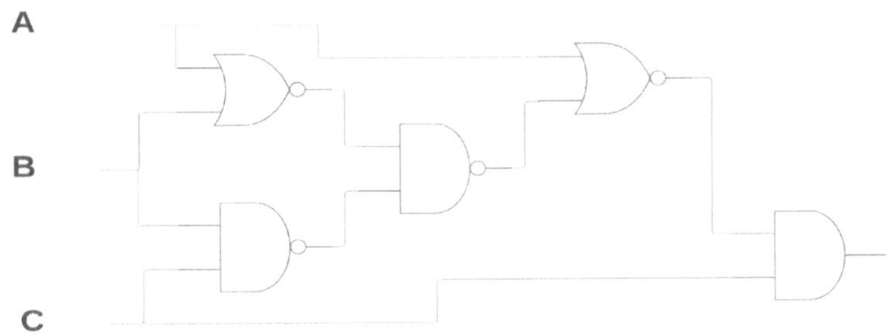

A

B

C

A. *01
B. 100
C. 0*0
D. 001
E. None of the above

8. Digital Electronics

Define a new gate , ☐ , with 3 inputs. It is TRUE if there is exactly one TRUE input. How many ordered triples make the following digital circuit TRUE?

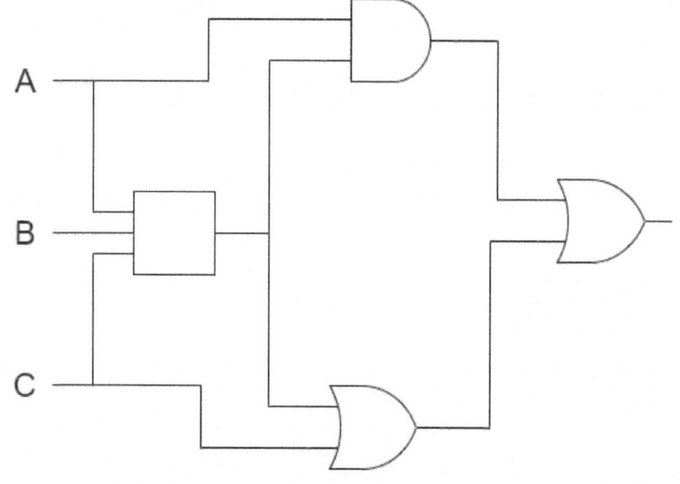

A. 0
B. 2
C. 4
D. 6
E. None of the above

9. Prefix-Infix-Postfix

Define: a # b = minimum of {a,b}

a $ b = average of a and b

a& = absolute value of a

Evaluate this postfix expression if all numbers are single digits:

2 4 # 4 2 $ 5 - & + 8 2 $ 7 3 $ * - &

A. 25
B. 29
C. 27
D. 21
E. None of the above

10. Prefix-Infix-Postfix

Evaluate this prefix expression if a = 1, b=3, c=5, and d=2:

*** / + a * b c * a ^ d 3 ^ b - c * 3 a**

A. 9
B. 11
C. 17
D. 18
E. None of the above

11. Computer Number Systems

How many 1's are there in the binary representations of the decimal numbers 50 to 64 inclusive?

A. 56
B. 60
C. 62
D. 70
E. None of the above

12. Computer Number Systems

Evaluate and express the result in hexadecimal:

$$2020_8 - 202_8 - 20_8 + 2_8$$

A. 700
B. 1F0
C. 380
D. 160
E. None of the above

13. Data Structures

What would be the next item popped given the following initially empty queue?

PUSH(R), PUSH(H), PUSH(O), PUSH(D), POP(X), POP(X), PUSH(O), POP(X), PUSH(D), PUSH(E), PUSH(N), POP(X), PUSH(D), PUSH(R), POP(X), POP(X), PUSH(O), PUSH(N), POP(X), POP(X), POP(X)

A. D
B. E
C. N
D. R
E. None of the above

14. Data Structures

How many nodes have only a left child in the binary search tree for:

CORONAVIRUS

A. 4
B. 5
C. 6
D. 8
E. None of the above

15. Graph Theory

How many cycles are there in the graph represented by the given adjacency matrix?

$$\begin{bmatrix} 1 & 0 & 1 & 1 \\ 1 & 0 & 1 & 1 \\ 0 & 0 & 1 & 1 \\ 1 & 0 & 1 & 0 \end{bmatrix}$$

A. 7
B. 6
C. 5
D. 4
E. None of the above

16. Graph Theory

Which two vertices have the most paths of length 2 between them? Write a 2-character string with the starting vertex followed by the ending vertex.

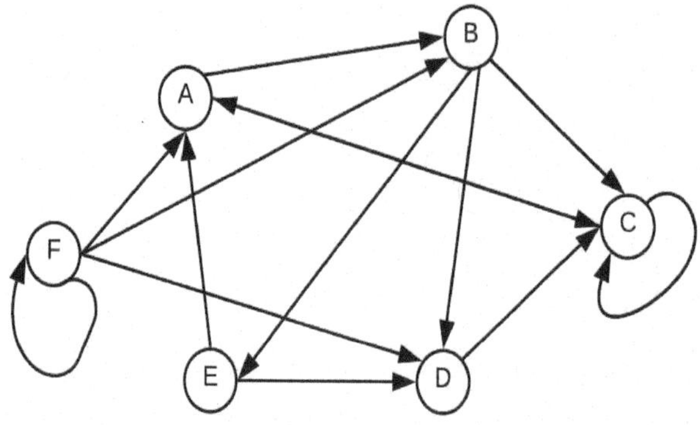

A. FA
B. AC
C. FC
D. BA
E. None of the above

17. What Does This Program Do?

What will be printed when this program is executed?

```
Y = 2020 : S = 0 : N = 0 : F = 0
for A = 1 to Y
    if INT(Y / A) == Y / A then
       S = S + A
       N = N + 1
   end if
   if S > Y and F = 0 then
       output N - 1
     F = 1
   end if
next
```

A. 8
B. 9
C. 10
D. 11
E. None of the above

18. LISP

After the following LISP program is run, what is the value of the last expression?

(SETQ Z '(C(O N)(N(E C)T)(I(C(U)T))))
(SETQ Y (CAR (REVERSE (CDR (CDR Z)))))
(CAR (CDR (CAR (CDR Y))))

A. (C (U) T)
B. (U)
C. ((U) T)
D. U
E. None of the above

19. FSAs and Regular Expressions

Given the regular expression:

[^aeiou]* [aeiou] [fghj-np-t] +. (ing|ful|age|less)?

Which of the following strings are accepted?

a. brush|ing	f. shapeless
b. help/ful	g. igloo
c. fractals	h. apple
d. java	i. striving
e. python!	j. image

A. a, b, d, e, f
B. a, c, d, e, g. h
C. a, b, e, f, h
D. b, d, e, f, h, j
E. None of the above

20. Assembly Language

How many different numbers are printed when the following program is run with input values 13, 24, 37, 45, 51, 60, 74, 0?

```
TOP     READ    N
        LOAD    N
        BE      STOP
        DIV     =10
        STORE   B
        MULT    =10
        STORE   X
        LOAD    N
        SUB     X
        STORE   C
        LOAD    B
        ADD     C
        STORE   M
        DIV     =3
        MULT    =3
        STORE   Y
        LOAD    M
        SUB     Y
        BE      DOWN
        BU      TOP
DOWN    LOAD    N
        PRINT   N
        BU      TOP
STOP    END
```

A. 4
B. 3
C. 2
D. 1
E. None of the above

American Computer Science League

2020 Finals • Solutions to Short Probs • Intermediate/Classroom Divisions

1. Boolean Algebra $\overline{A + \overline{\overline{B}}\, C} + \overline{B + \overline{A\, C}} + \overline{\overline{\overline{C}} + A\, B}$ $= \overline{A}\, \overline{\overline{B}\, C} + \overline{B}\, \overline{\overline{A\, C}} + \overline{\overline{C}}\, \overline{A\, B}$ $= \overline{A}(B + \overline{C}) + \overline{B}(A\, C) + C(\overline{A} + \overline{B})$ $= \overline{A}\, B + \overline{A}\, \overline{C} + A\, \overline{B}\, C + \overline{A}\, C + \overline{B}\, C$ $= \overline{A}\, B + \overline{A}(\overline{C} + C) + \overline{B}\, C\, (A + 1)$ $= \overline{A}\, B + \overline{A} + \overline{B}\, C$ $= \overline{A}(B + 1) + \overline{B}\, C$ $= \overline{A} + \overline{B}\, C$ There is 1 OR operator.	1. 1 (B)
2. Boolean Algebra First simplify the new operation: $A \$ B = \overline{A\, \overline{B} + \overline{A}}$ $= \overline{A\, \overline{B}}\, A$ $= (\overline{A} + B)\, A$ $= \overline{A}\, A + A\, B$ $= A\, B$ $A \$ B + B \$ C + \overline{A} \$ \overline{C}$ $= A\, B + B\, C + \overline{A}\, \overline{C}$ $If\ A = 0,\ then\ 0 + B\, C + \overline{C} = 0$ $\rightarrow \overline{C} = 0 \rightarrow C = 1 \wedge B = 0 \quad \Rightarrow (0, 0, 1)$ $If\ A = 1,\ then\ B + B\, C = 0$ $\rightarrow B = 0 \wedge C = 0\ or\ 1 \Rightarrow (1, 0, 1), (1, 0, 0)$	2. 3 (C)
3. Bit-String Flicking X = 01101 and Y = 10110 (RSHIFT-1 (LCIRC-3 X)) | (NOT (LSHIFT-1 ((RCIRC-2 X) & Y))) = (RSHIFT-1 (LCIRC-3 01101)) OR (NOT (LSHIFT-1 ((RCIRC-2 01101) AND 10110))) = (RSHIFT-1 01011) OR (NOT (LSHIFT-1 (01011 AND 10110))) = 00101 OR (NOT (LSHIFT-1 00010)) = 00101 OR (NOT 00100)	3. 11111 (A)

= 00101 OR 11011 = 11111	
4. Bit-String Flicking Let X = abcde and NOT X = ABCDE LHS = (LCIRC-2 01010) OR (RSHIFT-1 ((LCIRC-2 abcde) AND 01110)) = 01001 OR (RSHIFT-1 (cdeab AND 01110)) = (01001 OR (RSHIFT-1 0dea0) = 01001 OR 00dea = 01de1 LHS = RHS → 01de1 = 01101 → d = 1, e = 0, a = *, b = *, c = * → b = 1, c = 1, e = 1 → a = *, d = * Therefore X = abcde = ***10 8 solutions	4. 8 (C)
5. Recursive Functions $f(30) = f(30+3)+1 = f(33)+1 = 27+1 = 28$ $f(33) = 2\cdot f\left(\left[\frac{33}{2}\right]\right) - 3 = 2\cdot f(16) - 3 = 2\cdot 15 - 3 = 27$ $f(16) = 16 - 1 = 15$ $f(28) = 28 - 1 = 27$ $f(27) = 2\cdot f\left(\left[\frac{27}{2}\right]\right) - 3 = 2\cdot f(13) - 3 = 2\cdot 12 - 3 = 21$ $f(13) = 13 - 1 = 12$ $f(21) = 2\cdot f\left(\left[\frac{21}{2}\right]\right) - 3 = 2\cdot 9 - 3 = 15$ $f(10) = 10 - 1 = 9$ *So* $f(f(f(f(30))))$ $= f(f(f(28)))$ $= f(f(27))$ $= f(21)$ $= 15$	5. 15 (C)

6. Recursive Functions

$$f(14,20) = f(14+1, 20-2) + f(14,20) + 1$$

$$= f(15,18) + f(20,14) + 1 = 12 + 6 + 1 = 19$$

$$f(15,18) = f(15+1, 18-2) + f(18,15) + 1$$

$$= f(16,16) + f(18,15) + 1 = 8 + 3 + 1 = 12$$

$$f(20,14) = 20 - 14 = 6$$

$$f(16,16) = f\left(f\left(\frac{16}{2}, 16\right), \frac{16}{2}\right) - 3 = f(f(8,16), 8) - 3$$

$$= f(19,8) - 3 = 11 - 3 = 8$$

$$f(18,15) = 18 - 15 = 3$$

$$f(8,16) = f(8+1, 16-2) + f(16,8) + 1$$

$$= f(9,14) + f(16,8) + 1 = 10 + 8 + 1 = 19$$

$$f(9,14) = f(9+1, 14-2) + f(14,9) + 1$$

$$= f(10,12) + f(14,9) + 1 = 4 + 5 + 1 = 10$$

$$f(16,8) = 16 - 8 = 8$$

$$f(14,9) = 14 - 9 = 5$$

$$f(10,12) = f(10+1, 12-2) + f(12,10) + 1$$

$$= f(11,10) + f(12,10) + 1 = 1 + 2 + 1 = 4$$

$$f(11,10) = 11 - 10 = 1$$

$$f(12,10) = 12 - 10 = 2$$

$$f(19,8) = 19 - 8 = 11$$

6. 19 (A)

7. Digital Electronics

The digital circuit translates to:

$$\overline{\left(A + \overline{\overline{(A + B)}\,\overline{(B\,C)}}\right)}\,C$$

$$= \left(\overline{A}\left(\overline{A + B}\right)\left(\overline{B\,C}\right)\right)C$$

$$= (\overline{A}\,\overline{A}\,\overline{B}\,(\overline{B} + \overline{C}))\,C$$

$$= \overline{A}\,\overline{B}\,C\,(\overline{B} + \overline{C})$$

$$= \overline{A}\,\overline{B}\,C\,\overline{B} + \overline{A}\,\overline{B}\,C\,\overline{C}$$

$$= \overline{A}\,\overline{B}\,C + 0$$

$= \overline{A}\,\overline{B}\,C$ *which is TRUE if* $A = 0$, $B = 0$ *and* $C = 1$

7. 001 (D)

8. Digital Electronics

The circuit translates to:

(A)(☐(A, B, C) C) + ((☐(A, B, C) + C)

Let X = ☐ (A, B, C). The expression is now: A X + (X + C)

A	B	C	X	AX	X + C	AX + (X+C)
0	0	0	0	0	0	0
0	0	1	1	0	1	1
0	1	0	1	0	1	1
0	1	1	0	0	1	1
1	0	0	1	1	1	1
1	0	1	0	0	1	1
1	1	0	0	0	0	0
1	1	1	0	0	1	1

Therefore there are 6 triples that make the expression TRUE.

8. 6 (D)

9. Prefix-Infix-Postfix

2 4 # 4 2 $ 5 - & + 8 2 $ 7 3 $ * - &

= (2 4 #) (4 2 $) 5 - & + (8 2 $) (7 3 $) * - &

= 2 (3 5 -) & + (5 5 *) - &

= 2(-2 &) + 25 - &

= (2 2 +) 25 - &

= (4 25 -) &

= -21 &

= 21

9. 21 (D)

10. Prefix-Infix-Postfix

* / + a * b c * a ^ d 3 ^ b - c * 3 a

= * / + 1 (* 3 5) * 1 (^ 2 3) ^ 3 - 5 (* 3 1)

= * / (+ 1 15) (* 1 8) ^ 3 (- 5 3)

= * (/ 16 8) (^ 3 2)

= * 2 9

= 18

10. 18 (D)

11. Computer Number Systems

Change each to its binary representation:

50: 110010	55: 110111	60: 111100
51: 110011	56: 111000	61: 111101
52: 110100	57: 111001	62: 111110
53: 110101	58: 111010	63: 111111
54: 110110	59: 111011	64: 1000000

Therefore there are 60 1's.

11. 60 (B)

12. Computer Number Systems

$2020_8 - 202_8 - 20_8 + 2_8 = 1600_8$

Convert each bit to binary: 001 110 000 000

Group 4 at a time: 0011 1000 0000

Convert to hex: 3 8 0

12. 380 (C)

13. Data Structures

The queue is constructed using FIFO as follows:

R, RH, RHO, RHOD, ~~R~~HOD, HOD, ~~H~~OD, OD, ODO, ~~O~~DO. OD, ODD, ODDE, ODDEN, ~~O~~DDEN, DDEN, DDEND, DDENDR, ~~D~~DENDR, ~~D~~ENDR, ENDR, ENDRO, ENDRON, ~~E~~NDRON, NDRON, ~~N~~DRON, DRON, ~~D~~RON, RON. The next item popped would be R.

13. R (D)

14. Data Structures

The binary search tree is as follows:

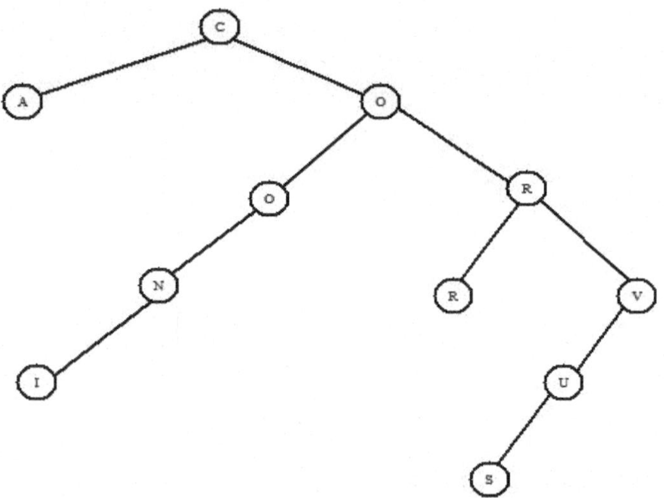

There are 4 nodes with only one left child: O, N, V, U

14. 4 (A)

15. Graph Theory

The graph that the adjacency matrix represents is:

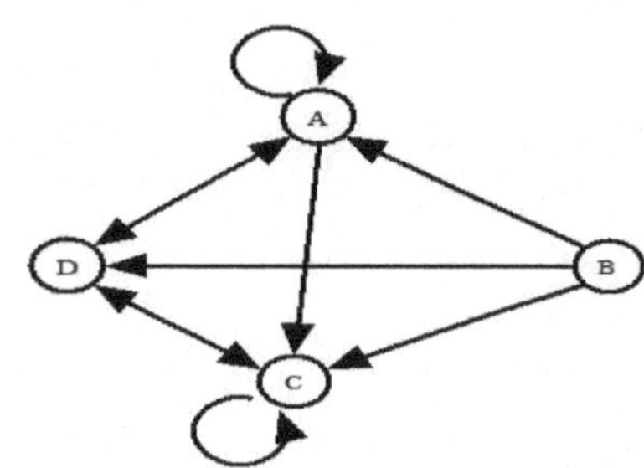

The cycles are: AA, ACDA, ADA, CC, and CDC.

15. 5 (C)

16. Graph Theory

$$\begin{bmatrix} 0 & 1 & 1 & 0 & 0 & 0 \\ 0 & 0 & 1 & 1 & 1 & 0 \\ 1 & 0 & 1 & 0 & 0 & 0 \\ 0 & 0 & 1 & 0 & 0 & 0 \\ 1 & 0 & 0 & 1 & 0 & 0 \\ 1 & 1 & 0 & 1 & 0 & 0 \end{bmatrix}^2 = \begin{bmatrix} 1 & 0 & 2 & 1 & 1 & 0 \\ 2 & 0 & 2 & 1 & 0 & 0 \\ 1 & 1 & 2 & 0 & 0 & 0 \\ 1 & 0 & 1 & 0 & 0 & 0 \\ 0 & 1 & 2 & 0 & 0 & 0 \\ 0 & 1 & 3 & 1 & 1 & 0 \end{bmatrix}$$

The starting and ending vertices with the most paths of length 2 between them are from F to C or FC.

16. FC (C)

17. What Does This Program Do? This program counts the number of increasing factors of 2020 that sum to less than 2020. They are 1, 2, 4, 5, 10, 20, 101, 202, 404 and 505.	17. 10 (C)
18. LISP (SETQ Z '(C(O N)(N(E C)T)(I(C(U)T)))) (CADADAR (REVERSE (CDDR Z))) (CDDR Z) = (CDDR '(C(O N)(N(E C)T)(I(C(U)T)))) = (CDR '((O N)(N(E C)T)(I(C(U)T)))) = '((N(E C)T)(I(C(U)T))) (REVERSE '((N(E C)T)(I(C(U)T)))) ='((I(C(U)T))(N(E C)T)) (CADADAR '((I(C(U)T))(N(E C)T))) = (CADADR '(I(C(U)T))) = (CADAR '((C(U)T))) = (CADR '(C(U)T)) = (CAR '((U)T)) = (U)	18. (U) (B)
19. FSAs and Regular Expressions `[^aeiou]* [aeiou] [fghj-np-t] +. (ing|ful|age|less)?` a. brush|ing - OK b. help/ful - OK c. fractals - fails at C d. java - fails at V e. python! - OK f. shapeless - OK g. igloo - fails at second o h. apple - OK i. striving - fails at v j. image - fails at g Therefore, there are 5 strings that satisfy the regular expression.	19. a, b, e, f, h (C)

20. Assembly Language

The assembly programs can be converted to ACSL WDTPD code as follows:

```
input n
while n != 0
   b = int(n / 10)
   x = b * 10
   c = n - x
   m = b + c
   y = m - int(m /  3) * 3
   if m == y then
      print n
   end if
   input n
end while
```

This program checks if a given number is divisible by 3 by adding the digits to see if the sum is a multiple of 3. There are 4 such numbers before inputting 0: 24, 45, 51, 60.

20. 4 (A)

American Computer Science League

2020 Finals • Solutions to Shorts Problems • Junior Division

1. Boolean Algebra

Simplify the following Boolean expression to use AND, OR, and NOT operators with no parentheses. How many OR operators are there?

$$\overline{A\overline{B} + C} \cdot A \cdot B \cdot \overline{\overline{B} + C}$$

A. 0
B. 1
C. 2
D. 3
E. None of the above

2. Boolean Algebra

Define a new binary operator, $, as follows:

$$A \,\$\, B = \overline{A}B + \overline{B}$$

It has higher precedence than the AND operator.

How many ordered pairs make the following TRUE?

$$A \,\$\, B + (\overline{A} + B)(\overline{A} \,\$\, \overline{B})$$

A. 0
B. 2
C. 3
D. 4
E. None of the above

3. Bit-String Flicking

Evaluate this expression:

```
(RSHIFT-2 (LCIRC-1 (NOT 0111001))) AND
(NOT (RCIRC-2 (LSHIFT-1 1100011)))
```

A. 1111101
B. 0101110
C. 0000010
D. 0000011
E. None of the above

4. Bit-String Flicking

How many different values of x (a bitstring of 5 bits) make the following equation true?

```
(LCIRC-2 01010) OR (RSHIFT-1 ((LCIRC-2 X) AND
              01110))= 01101
```

A. 0
B. 4
C. 8
D. 10
E. None of the above

5. Recursive Functions

Find f (17) given:

$$f(x) = \begin{cases} 2 \cdot f(x-3) + 4 & \text{if } x \geq 4 \\ 3x + 2 & \text{if } x < 4 \end{cases}$$

A. 8
B. 28
C. 124
D. 380
E. None of the above

6. Recursive Functions

Find f (25) given the function below if [x] is the greatest integer less than or equal to x:

$$f(x) = \begin{cases} 2 + f\left(\left[\dfrac{x}{2}\right]\right) & \text{if } x \geq 7 \\ f(x-1) + f(x-2) & \text{if } 3 < x < 7 \\ x^2 + 1 & \text{if } x \leq 3 \end{cases}$$

A. 25
B. 40
C. 44
D. 48
E. None of the above

7. Digital Electronics

Find all ordered triples that make the following circuit TRUE. Your answer will be a single 3-character string in the format XYZ where each X Y Z is either 0, 1, or * (e.g. 0*1, 110, **0).

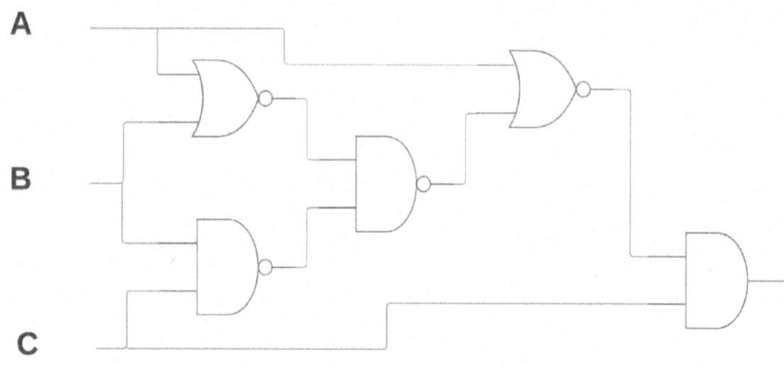

A. *01
B. 100
C. 0*0
D. 001
E. None of the above

8. Digital Electronics

Define a new gate , ☐ , with 3 inputs. It is TRUE if there is exactly one TRUE input. How many ordered triples make the following digital circuit TRUE?

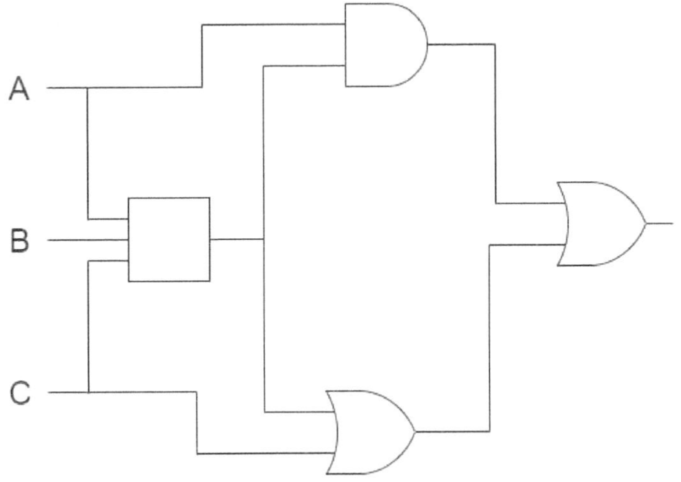

A. 0
B. 2
C. 4
D. 6
E. None of the above

9. Prefix-Infix-Postfix

Define: a $ b = minimum of {a,b}

a% = absolute value of a

Evaluate this prefix expression if all numbers are single digits:

- % - + 2 ^ 3 2 4 * + / 8 4 $ 2 0 / / + 8 2 $ 2 5 % - 3 8

A. 3
B. 5
C. 7
D. 9
E. None of the above

10. Prefix-Infix-Postfix

Evaluate the following postfix expression if A = 5, B = 3, and C = 2:

A B C + / B C ^ ^ B A + C B ^ / A * +

A. 6
B. 5
C. 1
D. -4
E. None of the above

11. Computer Number Systems

Evaluate and express the result in hexadecimal:

$$2020_8 - 202_8 - 20_8 + 2_8$$

A. 700
B. 1F0
C. 380
D. 160
E. None of the above

12. Computer Number Systems

How many 1's are there in the binary representations of the decimal numbers 50 to 64 inclusive?

A. 56
B. 60
C. 62
D. 70
E. None of the above

13. Data Structures

What would be the next item popped given the following initially empty stack?

PUSH(G), PUSH(E), PUSH(R), PUSH(B), POP(X), POP(X), PUSH(E), POP(X), PUSH(R), PUSH(A), PUSH(D), POP(X), PUSH(A), PUSH(I), POP(X), POP(X), PUSH(S), PUSH(Y), POP(X), POP(X), POP(X)

A. A
B. B
C. G
D. R
E. None of the above

14. Data Structures

What is the depth of the binary search tree for:

SOCIALDISTANCING

A. 4
B. 5
C. 6
D. 7
E. None of the above

15. Graph Theory

How many cycles are there in the graph represented by the given adjacency matrix?

$$\begin{bmatrix} 1 & 0 & 1 & 1 \\ 1 & 0 & 1 & 1 \\ 0 & 0 & 1 & 1 \\ 1 & 0 & 1 & 0 \end{bmatrix}$$

A. 7
B. 6
C. 5
D. 4
E. None of the above

16. Graph Theory

How many total paths of length 2 are in the following graph?

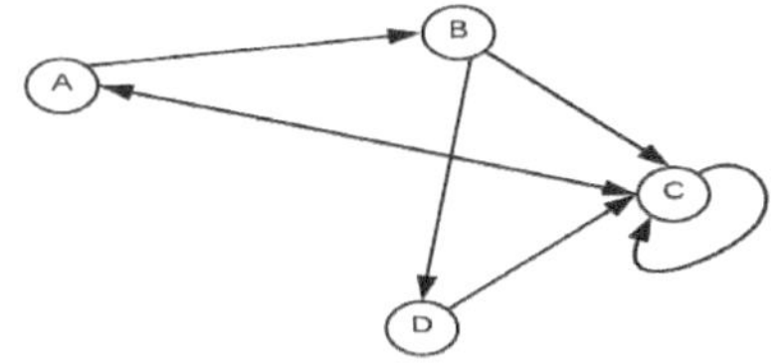

A. 10
B. 11
C. 12
D. 13
E. None of the above

17. What Does This Program Do?

What will be printed when this program is executed?

```
Y = 2020
S = 0 : N = 0 : F = 0
for A = 1 to Y
   if INT(Y / A) == Y / A then
       S = S + A
       N = N + 1
   end if
   if S > Y and F = 0 then
      output N - 1
      F = 1
   end if
next
```

A. 8
B. 9
C. 10
D. 11
E. None of the above

18. What Does This Program Do?

What will be printed when this program is executed? Remember A[0] = "C".

```
A = "CORONAVIRUS" : B = "COVID-19" : S = 0
for X = 0 to len(A) - 1
    for Y = 0 TO len(B) - 1
        if A[X] == B[Y] then
            S = S + X * Y
        end if
    next
next
output S
```

A. 16
B. 37
C. 40
D. 66
E. None of the above

19. What Does This Program Do?

What would be outputted when this program is executed on this predefined array of values (A)? Remember A(0) = 42.

42	19	71	21	28	69	33	57	11

```
S = 0 : N = 9
for X = 0 to N - 1
    S = S + A(X)
next
V = S / N
for X = 0 to N - 1
     if X < N / 2 and A(X) < V then
         C = C + 1
    else
        if X > N / 2 and A(X) > V then
            C = C + 1
        end if
    end if
next
output C
```

A. 0
B. 4
C. 5
D. 6
E, None of the above

20. What Does This Program Do?

What would be outputted when this program is executed given the following values of array A? Remember A(0,0) = 0.

Given the input values 4, 8, 11, 2, 5, 14, 6, what is the output?

0	3	2	4	1
4	5	1	3	2
1	2	4	5	1

```
S = 0
for N = 1 to 7
    input V
    R = int(V / 5)
    C = V % 5
    S = S + A(R,C)
next
output S
```

A. 18
B. 19
C. 21
D. 50
E. None of the above

American Computer Science League

2020 Finals • Solutions to Shorts Problems • Junior Division

---

1. Boolean Algebra

$\overline{A\,\overline{B} + C}\;A\,B\,\overline{\overline{B} + C}$

$= \overline{A\,\overline{\overline{B}}}\;\overline{C}\,A\,B\,B\,\overline{C}$

$= (\overline{A} + B)\;\overline{C}\,A\,B\,\overline{C}$

$= \overline{A}\,\overline{C}\,A\,B\,\overline{C} + B\,\overline{C}\,A\,B\,\overline{C}$

$= 0 + A\,B\,\overline{C}$

$= A\,B\,\overline{C}$ *which is TRUE if* $A = 1,\ B = 1,\ C = 0$

Answer: 1. 0 (A)

---

2. Boolean Algebra

First $A\ \$\ B = \overline{A}\,B + \overline{B}$

A \$ B + ($\overline{A}$ \$ B) ($\overline{A}$ \$ $\overline{B}$)

$= (\overline{A}\,B + \overline{B}) + \left(\overline{\overline{A}}\,B + \overline{B}\right)\left(\overline{\overline{A}}\,\overline{B} + \overline{\overline{B}}\right)$

$= (\overline{A}\,B + \overline{B}) + (A\,B + \overline{B})\,(A\,\overline{B} + B)$

$= (\overline{A}\,B + \overline{B}) + \left(A\,B\,A\,\overline{B} + A\,B\,B + \overline{B}\,A\,\overline{B} + \overline{B}\,B\right)$

$= \overline{A}\,B + \overline{B} + 0 + A\,B + A\,\overline{B} + 0$

$= B\,(\overline{A} + A) + \overline{B}\,(1 + A)$

$= B + \overline{B}$

$= 1$

This is always TRUE.

Answer: 2. 4 (D)

---

3. Bit-String Flicking

(RSHIFT-2 (LCIRC-1 (NOT 0111001))) AND
(NOT (RCIRC-2 (LSHIFT-1 1100011)))

= (RSHIFT-2 (LCIRC-1 1000110)) AND
(NOT (RCIRC-2 1000110))

= (RSHIFT-2 0001101) AND (NOT 1010001)

= 0000011 AND 0101110

= 0000010

Answer: 3. 0000010 (C)

---

4. Bit-String Flicking

Let X = abcde and NOT X = ABCDE

LHS = (LCIRC-2 01010) OR (RSHIFT-1 ((LCIRC-2 abcde)
AND 01110))

Answer: 4. 8 (C)

= 01001 OR (RSHIFT-1 (cdeab AND 01110)) = (01001 OR (RSHIFT-1 0dea0) = 01001 OR 00dea = 01de1 LHS = RHS → 01de1 = 01101 → d = 1, e = 0, a = *, b = *, c = * → b = 1, c = 1, e = 1 → a = *, d = * Therefore X = abcde = ***10 8 solutions	
5. Recursive Functions $f(17) = 2 \cdot f(17 - 3) + 4 = 2 \cdot f(14) + 4 = 2 \cdot 188 + 4 = 380$ $f(14) = 2 \cdot f(14 - 3) + 4 = 2 \cdot f(11) + 4 = 2 \cdot 92 + 4 = 188$ $f(11) = 2 \cdot f(11 - 3) + 4 = 2 \cdot f(8) + 4 = 2 \cdot 44 + 4 = 92$ $f(8) = 2 \cdot f(8 - 3) + 4 = 2 \cdot f(5) + 4 = 2 \cdot 20 + 4 = 44$ $f(5) = 2 \cdot f(5 - 3) + 4 = 2 \cdot f(2) + 4 = 2 \cdot 8 + 4 = 20$ $f(2) = 3 \cdot 2 + 2 = 8$	5. 380 (D)
6. Recursive Functions $f(25) = 2 + f\left(\left[\frac{25}{2}\right]\right) = 2 + f(12) = 2 + 42 = 44$ $f(12) = 2 + f\left(\left[\frac{12}{2}\right]\right) = 2 + f(6) = 2 + 40 = 42$ $f(6) = f(6 - 1) + f(6 - 2) = f(5) + f(4) = 25 + 15 = 40$ $f(5) = f(5 - 1) + f(5 - 2) = f(4) + f(3) = 15 + 10 = 25$ $f(4) = f(4 - 1) + f(4 - 2) = f(3) + f(2) = 10 + 5 = 15$ $f(3) = 3^2 + 1 = 10$ $f(2) = 2^2 + 1 = 5$	6. 44 (C)
7. Digital Electronics The digital circuit translates to:	7. 001 (D)

$$\overline{\left(A + \overline{\overline{(A + B)}\,\overline{(B\,C)}}\right)}\,C$$

$$= \left(\overline{A}\,\left(\overline{A + B}\right)\left(\overline{B\,C}\right)\right) C$$

$$= (\overline{A}\,\overline{A}\,\overline{B}\,(\overline{B} + \overline{C}))\,C$$

$$= \overline{A}\,\overline{B}\,C\,(\overline{B} + \overline{C})$$

$$= \overline{A}\,\overline{B}\,C\,\overline{B} + \overline{A}\,\overline{B}\,C\,\overline{C}$$

$$= \overline{A}\,\overline{B}\,C + 0$$

$$= \overline{A}\,\overline{B}\,C \textit{ which is TRUE if } A = 0,\ B = 0 \textit{ and } C = 1$$

8. Digital Electronics

The circuit translates to:

(A)(□(A, B, C)) + (((□ (A, B, C)) + C)

Let X = □ (A, B, C).

The expression is now: A X + (X + C)

A	B	C	X	AX	X + C	AX + (X+C)
0	0	0	0	0	0	0
0	0	1	1	0	1	1
0	1	0	1	0	1	1
0	1	1	0	0	1	1
1	0	0	1	1	1	1
1	0	1	0	0	1	1
1	1	0	0	0	0	0
1	1	1	0	0	1	1

Therefore there are 6 triples that make the expression TRUE.

8. 6 (D)

9. Prefix-Infix-Postfix

- % - + 2 ^ 3 2 4 * + / 8 4 $ 2 0 / / + 8 2 $ 2 5 % - 3 8

= - % - + 2 (^ 3 2) 4 * + (/ 8 4) ($ 2 0) / / (+ 8 2) ($ 2 5) % (- 3 8)

= - % - (+ 2 9) 4 * (+ 2 0) / (/ 10 2) (% (- 5))

= - % (- 11 4) * 2 (/ 5 5)

= - (% 7) (* 2 1)

= - 7 2 = 5

9. 5 (B)

10. Prefix-Infix-Postfix

If A = 5, B = 3, and C = 2:

A B C + / B C ^ ^ B A + C B ^ / A * +

= 5 3 2 + / 3 2 ^ ^ 3 5 + 2 3 ^ / 5 * +

= 5 (3 2 +) / (3 2 ^) ^ (3 5 +) (2 3 ^) / 5 * +

= (5 5 /) 9 ^ (8 8 /) 5 * +

= (1 9 ^) (1 5 *) +

= 1 5 +

= 6

10. 6 (A)

11. Computer Number Systems

$2020_8 - 202_8 - 20_8 + 2_8 = 1600_8$

Convert each bit to binary: 001 110 000 000

Group 4 at a time: 0011 1000 0000

Convert to hex: 3 8 0

11 380 (C)

12. Computer Number Systems

Change each to its binary representation:

50: 110010	55: 110111	60: 111100
51: 110011	56: 111000	61: 111101
52: 110100	57: 111001	62: 111110
53: 110101	58: 111010	63: 111111
54: 110110	59: 111011	64: 1000000

Therefore there are 60 1's.

12. 60 (B)

13. Data Structures

The stack is constructed using LIFO as follows:

G, GE, GER, GERB, GER~~B~~, GE~~R~~, GEE, GE~~E~~, GER, GERA, GERAD, GERA~~D~~, GERAA, GERAAI, GERAA~~I~~, GERA~~A~~, GERAS, GERASY, GERAS~~Y~~, GERA~~S~~, GER~~A~~

The next item popped would be R.

13. R (D)

14. Data Structures The binary search tree for SOCIALDISTANCING is: 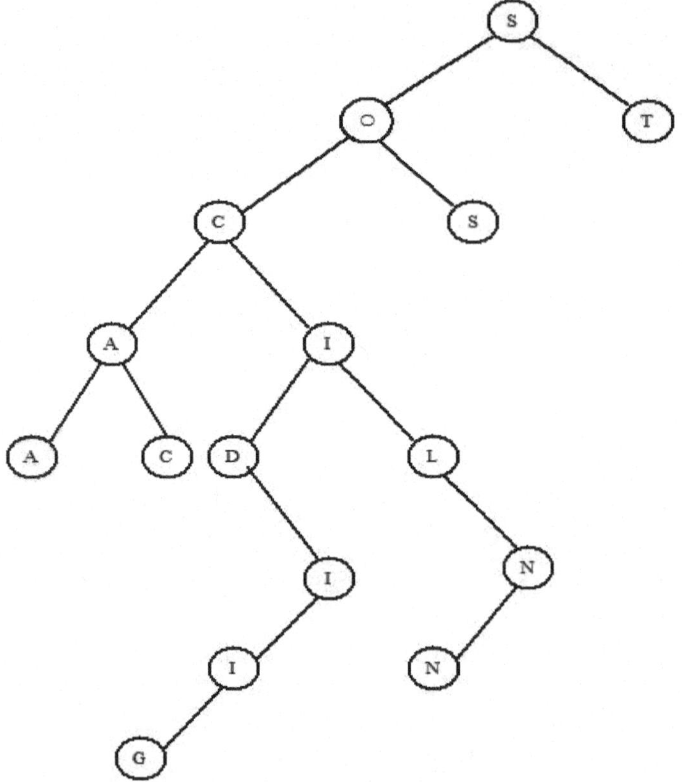 It has a depth of 7 since the root node has depth 0.	14. 7 (D)
15. Graph Theory The graph that the adjacency matrix represents is: 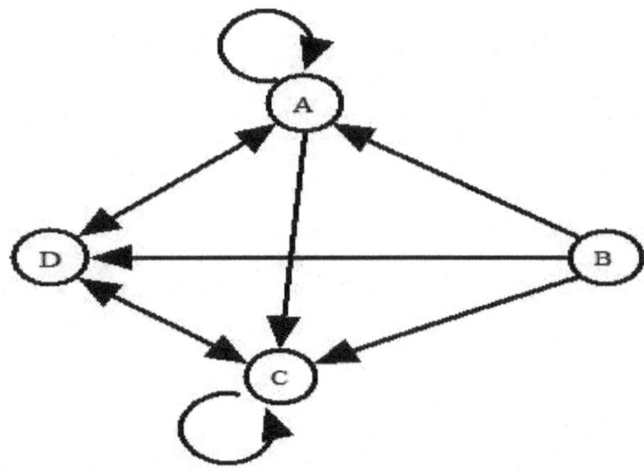 The cycles are: AA, ACDA, ADA, CC, and CDC.	15. 5 (C)

16. Graph Theoryoio

$$\begin{bmatrix} 0 & 1 & 1 & 0 \\ 0 & 0 & 1 & 1 \\ 1 & 0 & 1 & 0 \\ 0 & 0 & 1 & 0 \end{bmatrix}^2 = \begin{bmatrix} 1 & 0 & 2 & 1 \\ 1 & 0 & 2 & 0 \\ 1 & 1 & 2 & 0 \\ 1 & 0 & 1 & 0 \end{bmatrix}$$

By adding the entries in the squared matrix you get 13 paths of length 2.

16. 13 (D)

17. What Does This Program Do?

This program counts the number of increasing factors of 2020 that sum to less than 2020. They are 1, 2, 4, 5, 10, 20, 101, 202, 404 and 505.

17. 10 (C)

18. What Does This Program Do?

This program matches the letters in each string and sums the product of their locations.

Matching Letter	Position in A	Position in B	Sum
C	0	0	0
O	1	1	1
O	3	1	4
V	6	2	16
I	7	3	37

18. 37 (B)

19. What Does This Program Do?

This program adds all the entries in the array (352), then finds the average (39). It counts the entries in the first half that are less than the average (19, 21) and the entries in the upper half that are greater than the average (33, 11) and the middle entry (28). There are 5.

19. 5 (C)

20. What Does This Program Do?

This program finds the sum of specific input locations from 1 to 15.

N	V	R	C	A(R,C)	S
1	4	0	4	1	1
2	8	1	3	3	4
3	11	2	1	2	6
4	2	0	2	2	8
5	5	1	0	4	12
6	13	2	4	1	13
7	6	1	1	5	18

20. 18 (A)

American Computer Science League

2020 Finals • Shorts Problems • Elementary Division

1. Boolean Algebra

Determine which comparison symbol(s) could be used for the ? for the following expression to be TRUE.

NOT (10 - 3 ^ 2 ≤ 1) OR (56 / 8 - 1 ? 7 AND 4 + 5 * 2 > 13)

A. =
B. <
C. >
D. ≥
E. None of the above

2. Boolean Algebra

Simplify the following Boolean expression using the given symbols:

~(A + ~B) * ~AB + ~(A~B)

A. 1
B. ~A+B
C. ~AB
D. A+~B
E. None of the above

3. Boolean Algebra

Define a new binary operator, $, as follows:

A $ B = ~AB

It has higher precedence than the AND operator.

How many ordered pairs make the following TRUE?

A $ B + (~A $ B) (~A $ ~B)

A. 1
B. 2
C. 3
D. 4
E. None of the above

4. Prefix-Infix-Postfix

Evaluate the following postfix expression:

2 3 2 ^ * 4 - 8 4 / / 5 2 * 2 + 2 / *

A. 13
B. 42
C. 60
D. 96
E. None of the above

5. Prefix-Infix-Postfix Evaluate the following prefix expression if all numbers are single digits: **+ / * 4 + 2 7 ^ 6 2 * ^ + 1 4 2 2**	A. 21 B. 86 C. 50 D. 51 E. None of the above
6. Prefix-Infix-Postfix Define: a $ b = minimum of {a,b} a # b = maximum of {a,b} Evaluate this prefix expression if all numbers are single digits: **/ # * - ^ 3 2 4 7 ^ 6 $ 2 8 4**	A. 7 B. 9 C. 11 D. 13 E. None of the above
7. Computer Number Systems Evaluate and express the result in hexadecimal: $\mathbf{2020_8 - 202_8 - 20_8 + 2_8}$	A. F00 B. 700 C. 380 D. 3A0 E. None of the above
8. Computer Number Systems How many 1's are there in the binary representations of the decimal numbers 16 to 32 inclusive?	A. 48 B. 49 C. 50 D. 52 E. None of the above

9. Computer Number Systems

Which of the following has the smallest value in base 10?

a. $4A_{16}$ b. 1001001_2 c. 112_8 d. 49_{16} e. 110_8

A. $4A_{16}$
B. 1001001_2
C. 112_8
D. 49_{16}
E. 110_8

10. Graph Theory

Determine if the graph is traversable. Your answer should be NO, YES if any pair of vertices could work, or the only possible starting and ending vertex in alphabetical order (e.g. AB, not BA).

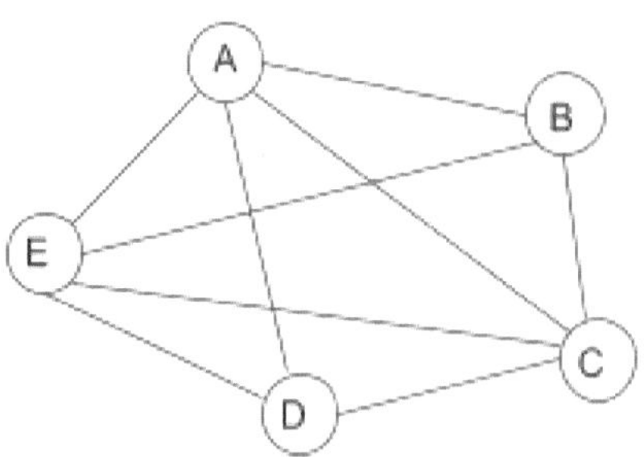

A. NO
B. AE
C. BD
D. YES
E. None of the above

11. Graph Theory

How many cycles are there in the graph represented by the graph defined by vertices {A,B,C,D} and edges {AB,BD,CA,DC}?

A. 0
B. 2
C. 4
D. 8
E. None of the above

12. Graph Theory

Determine the number of simple paths that exist from vertex A to vertex D.

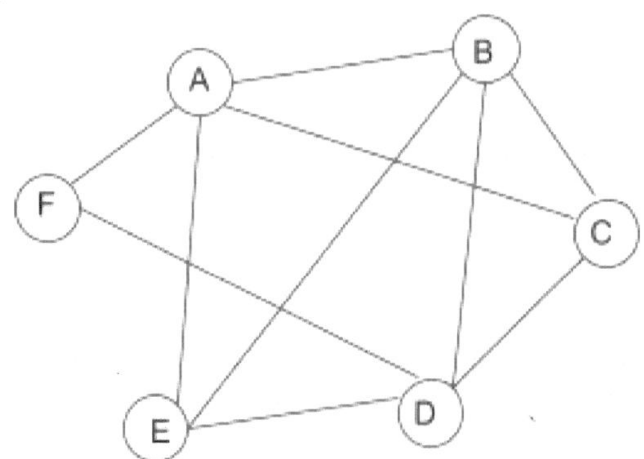

A. 7
B. 8
C. 9
D. 10
E. None of the above

American Computer Science League

2020 Finals • Solutions to Shorts Problems • Elementary Division

1. Boolean Algebra NOT (10 - 3 ^ 2 ≤ 1) = NOT(1 ≤ 1) = NOT (true) = false Therefore, the other expression must be true for OR to be true. 4 + 5 * 2 > 13 is the same as 14 > 13 which is always true. Therefore, 56 / 8 - 1 ? 7 means 6 ? 7 must be true for AND to be true. 6 < 7 is the only option. That gives the correct solution: false OR (true AND true) = true.	1. < (B)
2. Boolean Algebra ~(A + ~B) * ~AB + ~(A~B) = (~A + ~(~B)) * ~AB + ~A + ~(~B) = ~A(~AB) + B(~AB) + ~A + B = ~AB + ~AB + ~A + B = ~AB + ~A + B You may use either ~A(B + 1) + B = ~A + B or B(~A + 1) + ~A = B + ~A. The only possible answer is ~A + B which is choice b.	2. ~A+B (B)
3. Boolean Algebra If A $ B = ~AB, then A $ B + (~A $ B) (~A $ ~B) = ~AB + (~(~A) B) (~(~A) (~B)) = ~AB + (AB) (A~B) = ~AB + A(~B)(B) = ~AB + A(0) = ~AB Therefore, there is 1 solution: (0,1).	3. 1 (A)
4. Prefix-Infix-Postfix 2 3 2 ^ * 4 - 8 4 / / 5 2 * 2 + 2 / * = ((((2 (3 2 ^) *) 4 -) (8 4 /) /) (((5 2 *) 2 +) 2 /) *) = ((((2 9 *) 4 -) 2 /) ((10 2 +) 2 /) *) = (((18 4 -) 2 /) (12 2 /) *)	4. 42 (B)

= ((14 2 /) 6 *) = (7 6 *) = 42	
5. Prefix-Infix-Postfix + / * 4 + 2 7 ^ 6 2 * ^ + 1 4 2 2 = (+ (/ (* 4 (+ 2 7)) (^ 6 2)) (* (^ (+ 1 4) 2) 2)) = (+ (/ (* 4 9) 36) (* (^ 5 2) 2)) = (+ (/ 36 36) (* 25 2)) = (+ 1 50) = 51	5. 51 (D)
6. Prefix-Infix-Postfix / # * - ^ 3 2 4 7 ^ 6 $ 2 8 4 = (/ (# (* (- (^ 3 2) 4) 7) (^ 6 ($ 2 8))) 4) = (/ (# (* (- 9 4) 7) (^ 6 2)) 4) = (/ (# (* 5 7) 36) 4) = (/ (# 35 36) 4) = (/ 36 4) = 9	6. 9 (B)
7. Computer Number Systems $2020_8 - 202_8 - 20_8 + 2_8 = 1616_8 - 20_8 + 2_8 = 1576_8 + 2_8 = 1600_8$ Remember, when subtracting in base 8, you must borrow 8, not 10. Also, when adding in base 8, you must carry 8 which occurs twice. 1600_8 = 001 110 000 000 = 11 1000 0000 = 380_{16}	7. 380 (C)
8. Computer Number Systems The 4 digits for all hexadecimal numbers are 0000=0, 0001=1, 0010=1, 0011=2, 0100=1, 0101=2, 0110 = 2, 0111=3 or a total of 12 for the first 8 and another 12+8 for the second 8. That equals 32. The numbers 16 to 31 have an additional 16 1's at the beginning for a total of 48. The number 32=100000 which makes 49.	8. 49 (B)

9. Computer Number Systems a. $4A_{16} = 4 * 16 + 10 = 74_{10}$ b. $1001001_2 = 1 + 8 + 64 = 73_{10}$ c. $112_8 = 1 * 64 + 1 * 8 + 2 = 74_{10}$ d. $49_{16} = 4 * 16 + 0 = 73_{10}$ e. $110_8 = 64 + 8 = 72_{10}$	9. 110_8 (E)
10. Graph Theory The degree on each vertex is: A = 4, B = 3, C = 4, D = 3, and E = 4. Traversable graphs are possible when there are either 0 or 2 vertices with an odd degree. Because there are 2 of them, all possible paths must start with B or D and end at the other vertex. One path is BCABEADCED, but others are possible. The vertices must be listed alphabetically as BD. 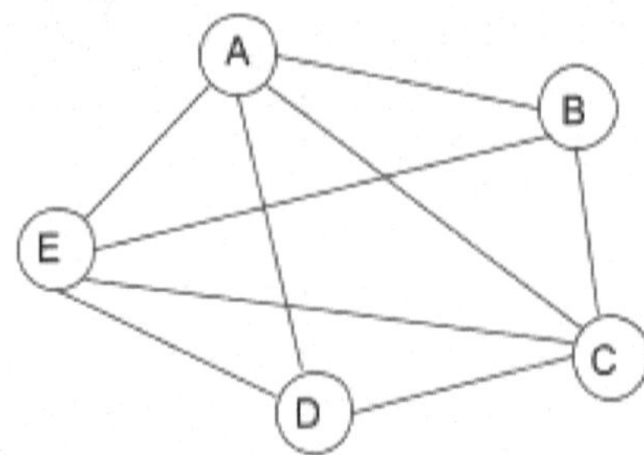 	10. BD (C)
11. Graph Theory The graph can be drawn as follows. From vertex A, the 2 cycles are ABDCA and ACDBA. There are no cycles using just 3 vertices and all others from another vertex are the same path. 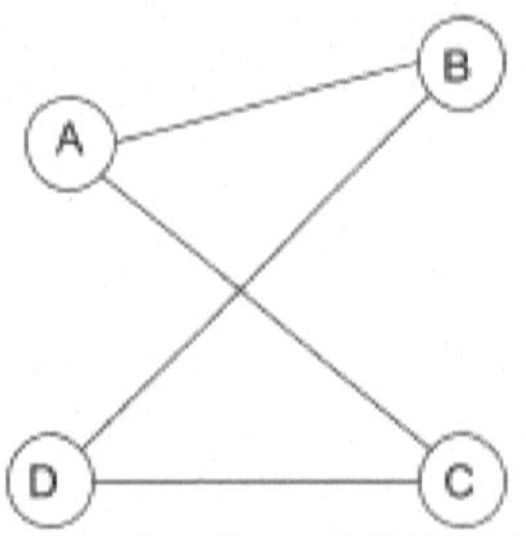 	11. 2 (B)

12. Graph Theory

By inspection, there is no direct path from A to D. There are 4 paths of length 2: ABD, ACD, AED, and AFD. There are 4 paths of length 3: ABCD, ABED, ACBD, and AEBD. There are 2 paths of length 4: ACBED and AEBCD. There are none of length 5 which would include all 6 vertices. That's a total of 10.

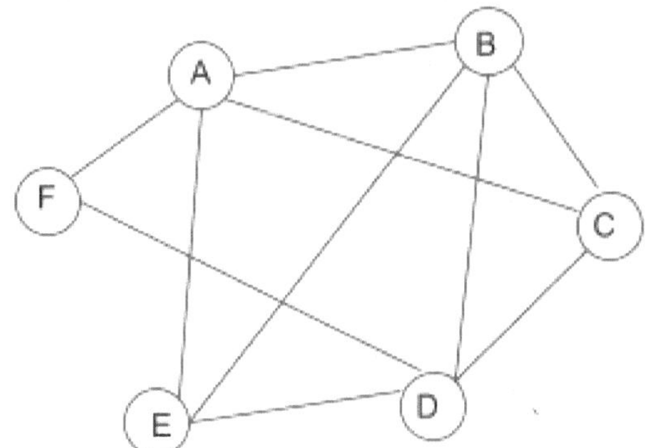

12. 10 (D)

American Computer Science League

2020 Finals • Program 4: Family Tree • Senior Division

PROBLEM: Given a set of parent-child relationships, report how two individuals are related. Consider the following set of parent-child relationships:

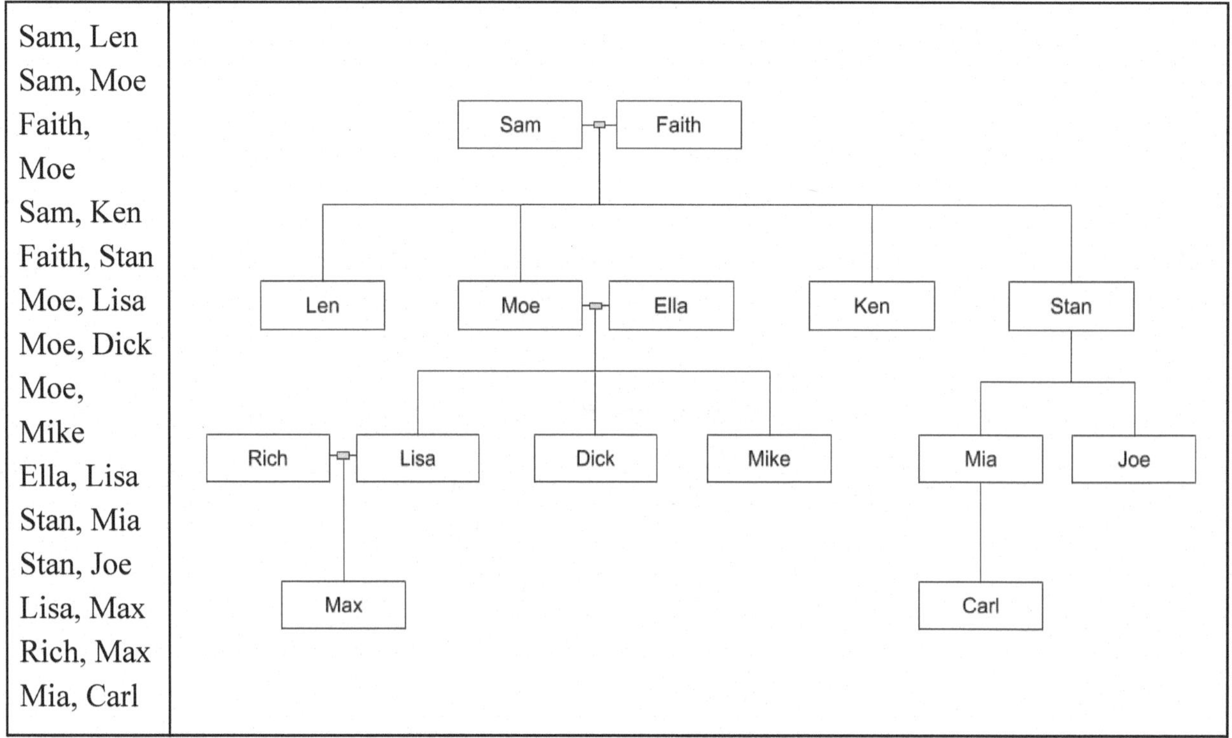

Sam is married to Faith; they have 4 children: Len, Moe, Ken, and Stan. Moe is married to Ella, and they have 3 children: Lisa, Dick, and Mike. Lisa is married to Rich and has one child, Max. Stan has two children: Mia and Joe. Mia has one child: Carl, and there is no spouse given for Mia or for Stan.

Because we are not giving the gender of any person, we will use *pibling* rather than aunts and uncles, and *nibling* rather than nieces and nephews. Also, there is no distinction between "in-laws". For example, Ella, the spouse of Moe, has the exact same parents, siblings, etc. as Moe has.

Here are examples of the relationship of two people in the example above:

Sam is Moe's parent
Faith is Mike's grandparent
Lisa is Sam's grandchild
Dick and Mia are cousins
Rich and Joe are cousins
Dick is Max's nibbling
Carl and Max are second cousins
Sam is Carl's great-grandparent

American Computer Science League

2020 Finals • Program 4: Family Tree • Senior Division

We guarantee that the input data will be a valid family tree with at most 10 generations. All siblings have the same parents, and a parent will have no more than 5 children. A person has at most 2 parents, and siblings cannot marry each other.

The relationships that will be tested are as follows:

- **spouse**
- **parent, grandparent, great-grandparent** - direct lineage
- **child, grandchild, great-grandchild** - direct lineage
- **sibling** - individuals with the same parents
- **cousin** - individuals whose parents are siblings
- **second cousin** - individuals whose parents are cousins
- **pibling**- Tom is a pibling of Bob, if Tom is a sibling of one of Bob's parents
- **grandpibling** - Ann is a grandpibling of Bob, if Ann is a sibling of one of Bob's grandparents
- **nibling** - Fran is a nibling of Betty, if one of Fran's parents is a sibling of Betty
- **grandnibling** - Ned is a grandnibling of Joy, if one of Ned's grandparents is a sibling of Joy

INPUT: A set of family trees with relationships to report about each tree. For each data set, there will be a number representing how many parent-child relationships to read in followed by the family tree data which is a set of parent-child relationships, one relationship per line. This will be followed by a number representing the number of outputs requested. For each output requested, the relationships data will be a pair of names in the family tree, one relationship per line.

OUTPUT: For each relationship line, report the relationship of the second person to the first. There will be 10 relationships to report. We guarantee that the relationship will be one of the above.

Output is being scored by a computer, so you must print the relationships exactly as they appear above: all lowercase letters, spelled as above, a single space between the words in *second cousin*, a dash (with no spaces) in *great-grandparent*, and *great-grandchild.*

The Sample Data below shows 3 family trees. The first one is a tree with 5 people. The 2nd and 3rd are the tree above, with the relationships expressed differently.

American Computer Science League

2020 Finals • Program 4: Family Tree • Senior Division

SAMPLE INPUT (shown in 3 columns):

```
4
Moe Lisa
Moe Dick
Moe Mike
Ella Mike
2
Moe Ella
Mike Ella
```

```
14
Sam Len
Sam Moe
Faith Moe
Sam Ken
Faith Stan
Moe Lisa
Moe Dick
Moe Mike
Ella Lisa
Stan Mia
Stan Joe
Lisa Max
Rich Max
Mia Carl
4
Dick Max
Mike Faith
Faith Mike
Carl Ken
```

```
14
Ella Lisa
Mia Carl
Ella Dick
Lisa Max
Faith Ken
Rich Max
Sam Ken
Moe Lisa
Sam Stan
Stan Mia
Sam Moe
Faith Len
Ella Mike
Stan Joe
4
Max Carl
Mike Joe
Rich Mike
Dick Stan
```

SAMPLE OUTPUT:

1. spouse
2. parent
3. nibling
4. grandparent
5. grandchild
6. grandpibling
7. second cousin
8. cousin
9. sibling
10. pibling

American Computer Science League

2020 Finals • Program 4: Family Tree • Senior Division

TEST INPUT (shown in 3 columns):

10
Pat Rich
Rich Jo
Pat Robin
Sam Rich
Pat Quinn
Robin Dale
Robin Bobby
Noel Bobby
Jo Lynn
Quinn Max
2
Sam Lynn
Bobby Sam

10
Robin Dale
Pat Robin
Sam Rich
Pat Quinn
Pat Rich
Robin Bobby
Noel Bobby
Jo Lynn
Quinn Max
Rich Jo
3
Quinn Lynn
Lynn Sam
Dale Jo

20
Zion Pat
Zion Rich
Rich Hayden
Pat Max
Logan Pat
Zion Wyatt
Wyatt Quinn
Quinn Robin
Terry Max
Hayden Alex
Alex Noel
Faith Robin
Quinn Kaden
Max Jesse
Robin Brook
Sam Noel
Max Dale
Sam Emory
Quinn Val
Noel Gabriel
5
Val Robin
Rich Emory
Jesse Wyatt
Dale Robin
Pat Kaden

TEST OUTPUT:

1. great-grandchild
2. grandparent
3. grandnibling
4. great-grandparent
5. cousin
6. sibling
7. great-grandchild
8. grandpibling
9. second cousin
10. grandnibling

American Computer Science League

2020 Finals • Program 3: Syllables • Intermediate/Senior Divisions

PROBLEM: *Given a word, separate it into syllables following the ACSL rules.*

Words consist of *vowels* (a, e, i, o, and u) and *consonants* (all other letters). The letter y is always considered a consonant. There are *combo consonants* (ch, ck, ph, sh, th, wh, wr) that are treated as a single consonant and never separated. A word may also have a *prefix* (co, de, dis, pre, re, un) and/or a *suffix* (age, ful, ing, less, ment).

A *syllable* is a unit of pronunciation having one vowel sound, with or without surrounding consonants, forming the whole or a part of a word. For example, there are two syllables in 'cater': ca|ter. There are three syllables in 'inferno': in|fer|no.

To separate a word into its syllables, use the following rules. These rules are pretty similar to English, but not the same. Follow these rules and these rules only!

Separate the word into syllables using the following 4 rules:

1. Separate the prefix, if any. For example, "pre|paid" and "re|port".
2. Separate the suffix, if any. For example, "end|less" and "help|ing".
3. After removing the prefix and suffix, find any single consonants and split before the consonant. For example, "o|pen" , "pa|per", and "o|ther". Note there must be one or more vowels both before and after the consonant. Combo-consonants (e.g., the "th") are considered as a single consonant.
4. After removing the prefix and suffix, find any double consonants and split in the middle. For example, "hap|pen" , "bas|ket", "kick|ball", and "back|wraps".

We guarantee that there will be no more than 2 consonants in a row. The words "kickball" and "backwraps" are legal because the "th" and the "ck" are combo-consonants, but "string" is not valid.

INPUT: There will be 10 inputs. Each input is a word, a string of lowercase letters.

OUTPUT: For each input, break the word into syllables by inserting a '|' between syllables. Then print the sum of the location(s) of each '|' starting with position 0 for the first character in the string. For all one-syllable words, the answer should be 0.

SAMPLE INPUT:	**SAMPLE OUTPUT: (print the number only!)**	
choice	1. 4	`choi|ce`
rewriting	2. 9	`re|writ|ing`
seashell	3. 3	`sea|shell`

American Computer Science League

2020 Finals • Program 3: Syllables • Intermediate/Senior Divisions

TEST DATA

TEST INPUT:

blackberries
unimaginable
antidisestablishment
trigonometric
dealphabetized
disintegration
irregardless
tablespoonful
prelanguage
cobushwhacker

TEST OUTPUT (the word shows how the answer is found; it should not be printed)

1. 14 black|ber|ries
2. 37 un|i|ma|gi|nab|le
3. 64 an|ti|di|ses|tab|lish|ment
4. 31 tri|go|no|met|ric
5. 43 de|al|pha|be|ti|zed
6. 32 dis|in|teg|ra|tion
7. 17 ir|re|gard|less
8. 22 tab|les|poon|ful
9. 20 pre|lan|gu|age
10. 20 co|bush|wha|cker

American Computer Science League

2020 Finals • Program 2: Passort • Junior/Intermediate Divisions

PROBLEM: The Passort algorithm for sorting a string operates as follows:

1. Find the smallest character not in its correct final position. Swap it with the character where it belongs. Use the first occurrence when characters are the same.

2. Find the largest character not in its correct final position. Swap it with the character where it belongs. Use the last occurrence when characters are the same.

3. Repeat steps 1 and 2 until the string is sorted.

Characters are compared based on their ASCII codes: numbers, then upper case letters, and finally lowercase letters.

EXAMPLE: A S O R T I N G

pass 1: smallest character not in position is the G swap it with the S: A **G** O R T I N **S**
pass 2: largest character not in position is the T swap it with the S: A G O R **S** I N **T**
pass 3: smallest character not in position is the I swap it with the O: A G **I** R S **O** N T
pass 4: largest character not in position is the S swap it with the N: A G I R **N** O **S** T
pass 5: smallest character not in position is the N swap it with the R: A G I **N** **R** O S T
pass 6: largest character not in position is the R swap it with the O: A G I N **O** **R** S T

At this point, the string is sorted so we are done. There were 6 swaps.

INPUT: There will be 10 lines of data. Read each line as a string.

OUTPUT: Run Passort on each input string after all non-alphanumeric characters have been deleted from the string. Print the number of swaps made during the execution.

SAMPLE INPUT:	**SAMPLE OUTPUT:**
ASORTING	1. 6
10 Java Programs	2. 11
CONNECTICUT - CT	3. 9

American Computer Science League

2020 Finals • Program 2: Passort • Junior/Intermediate Divisions

TEST DATA

TEST INPUT:

ASORTINGALGORITHM
ACSL All-Star Contest
0123456789BDFHJLNPRTVXZacegikmoqsuwx
ZYXWVUTSRQPONMLKJIHGFEDCBA
AP COMPUTER SCIENCE PRINCIPLES is abbreviated AP CSP
American Computer Science League uses ACSL
IT'S A BEAUTIFUL DAY IN THE NEIGHBORHOOD
CONNECTICUT is the CONSTITUTION STATE!
APPLE,BANANA,GRAPE,PEACH,PEAR,ORANGE,GUAVA,PAPAYA,MANGO,KIWI,PINEAPPLE
There are 10 Kinds of People in the World, Those Who Know Binary and Those Who Don't.

TEST OUTPUT:

1. 11
2. 12
3. 0
4. 13
5. 36
6. 30
7. 27
8. 31
9. 52
10. 58

American Computer Science League

2020 Finals • Program 1: Spot the Y • Junior Division

●	2	●	4	5
6	●	■	9	10
11	●	13	■	■
16	17	■	19	20
21	22	23	24	25

1	2	3	4	■
6	7	■	■	10
11	●	13	14	■
16	●	18	19	20
●	22	●	24	25

PROBLEM: *Spot-The-Y* is a game played by 2 players on an N x N grid. The grid squares are numbered as above, with 1 is in the upper left corner, and N^2 is in the lower right corner. Players in turn place a marker (circles for the first player and squares for the second player) in an empty grid space or remove one of their own markers from the grid. The winner is the first player to create a "Y" with his own markers.

A "Y" pattern has two markers adjacent horizontally or vertically, and two other markers diagonally connected to one of the adjacent ones. The grids above show the 4 possible orientations of a "Y" pattern.

INPUT: There will be 10 lines of data with each representing a game of *Spot-The-Y.* Each line will contain an integer, *N*, giving the size of the square grid. That will be followed by a series of integers (1 through N^2), giving the moves of the two players in alternating order. If the move directs a player to a grid square that is empty, that player places his marker in that square. If the grid square contains his marker, it is removed. There will not be any input where the grid square is occupied by an opponent's marker.

OUTPUT: For each game, print the sum of the grid square numbers that produced the first "Y" found. If there is no Y found after all of the moves, print 0.

SAMPLE INPUT:

```
5 1 14 12 18 3 15 7 8
5 1 14 24 20 12 18 3 15 12 20 17 8
6 23 1 21 5 23 8 14 36 16 12 27 7
```

SAMPLE OUTPUT:

1. 23
2. 55
3. 78

American Computer Science League

2020 Finals • Program 1: Spot the Y • Junior Division

TEST DATA

TEST INPUT:

```
5 8 1 25 24 25 11 8 7 22 19 15 8 22 16 21 3
6 25 21 13 15 20 10 27 1 14 3 32 28 9 36 14 29 22  1
6 36 24 29 22 17 11 29 27 17 27 34 17 23 35 29
8 3 10 46 12 3 13 37 12 54 19 39 27 39 12
8 12 1 19 10 3 17 19 1 5 2 28 19 28 17 20
4 3 5 10 11 10 12 6 10 1 14 13 12 4 14 14 7 9 11 8 2 8 11 13 15
7 10 31 15 23 18 25 16 45 18 30 46 38 24 25 15 25 32 22 10
9 10 20 30 2 4 6 8 3 9 12 15 18 21 24 27 5 25 7 14 11 17 1
10 99 88 80 78 69 97 60 68 99 78 67 68 67 78 68 99
3 1 2 3 4 5 6 7 8 9 8 7 6 5 4 3 2 1 1 3 5 7 8 6 4 2 5 5
```

TEST OUTPUT:

1. 27
2. 86
3. 74
4. 176
5. 48
6. 0
7. 117
8. 77
9. 277
10. 23